R.H.R

Rambles in Istria, Dalmatia and Montenegro

R.H.R

Rambles in Istria, Dalmatia and Montenegro

ISBN/EAN: 9783337241155

Printed in Europe, USA, Canada, Australia, Japan

Cover: Foto ©Andreas Hilbeck / pixelio.de

More available books at **www.hansebooks.com**

RAMBLES IN ISTRIA,

DALMATIA AND MONTENEGRO.

BY

R. H. R.

" Dirvi ch' io sia, saria parlar indarno."—DANTE.

IN ONE VOLUME.

LONDON:
HURST AND BLACKETT, PUBLISHERS.
13, GREAT MARLBOROUGH STREET.
1875.

PREFACE.

EVERY year more and more is the constantly recurring question ever put "Where shall we go to this Summer?" and every year the field for selection gets narrower and narrower.

In writing the following pages, my object has been less to make a book than to point out to those who are tired of the old beaten tracks, countries within easy reach of London, but seldom visited, and quite outside the lines affected by the typical tourist:—countries where at moderate expense and with total freedom from danger they may enjoy new scenery, receive fresh impressions, acquire new information; and if by so doing I shall have suggested to others one more field for exploration that shall afford them half the enjoyment which I experienced during my wanderings, I shall consider myself very amply rewarded.

CONTENTS.

CHAPTER I.

CHAPTER II.

CHAPTER III.

CHAPTER IV.

CHAPTER V.

CHAPTER VI.

CHAPTER VII.

CHAPTER VIII.

CHAPTER IX.

CHAPTER X.

CHAPTER XI.

CHAPTER XII.

CHAPTER XIII.

CHAPTER XIV.

CHAPTER XV.

CHAPTER XVI.

CHAPTER XVII.

CHAPTER XVIII.

CHAPTER XIX.

CHAPTER XX.

CHAPTER XXI.

CHAPTER XXII.

RAMBLES IN ISTRIA, DALMATIA,

AND

MONTENEGRO.

CHAPTER I.

A CONVERSATION—WHERE SHALL WE GO FOR A HOLIDAY TRIP —ATTRACTIONS OF LAPLAND—REMINISCENCES OF ITALY— THE GRAND TOUR IN FORMER DAYS—HOW TO STUDY HISTORY —DIFFICULTY OF FINDING NEW GROUND FOR TRAVEL—AN INTERESTING COUNTRY WITHIN FIVE DAYS OF TEMPLE BAR.

"LET us go to Lapland!" was the exclamation which rang on my ear, as I was entering my club, one fine morning in the early part of June, 1873.

"Lapland!" said I, "what put that into your head?"

" Yes," replied my friend M——, in his rich, good-humoured voice, slightly flavoured with Hibernian Doric. "I hear that somebody has written a book about it. I have been everywhere else in Europe—and it is quite the place to go to now, you know. We shall pic-nic on Cape North and then drive across to Spitzbergen in reindeer sledges on the ice, it will be awfully jolly !" and his joyous laugh echoed through the hall. "Do come, like a good fellow," said he, "there will be just the four of us, R——, C——, yourself, and I, and you really must not say no, for we none of us can speak a word of anything but English, while you speak every language under the sun. So agree to it at once ; let us all meet here to dinner, to-morrow at six, and then off by the mail to Calais."

At first I thought that M—— was chaffing ; but having now been joined by R—— and C——, who at once chimed in on the same subject, I said,

" Have you any idea about Lapland, my dear M——, do you know anything about it? and what do you expect to see there ?"

"Oh, dear me, yes," replied he, "it is a country in the North of Europe, surrounded on all sides either by land or by water, and inhabited by men who are four feet six high, and the darlingest little women just four feet nothing. They go to church on Sundays, riding on reindeer, and shoot Polar bears with bows and arrows! Oh dear, yes, I know all about Lapland."

"Not at all a bad account," said I, "but what writes Captain Hutchinson in his book? Is his description of Lapland very captivating?"

"Well," answered M——, "I confess I have not read his book; but go abroad I must, London is getting too stupid, and I have been everywhere else in Europe; and I want to see a country out of the beaten track, something I have not yet seen."

"Now, my dear fellow," said I, "though I have not been exactly in Lapland, I have been in Finland, and that, you know, is just next door to it; and knowing what the mosquitoes are in those swampy northern latitudes, nothing could induce me to visit those countries again in Summer, except for very cogent reasons indeed. But come now, tell me where have you been, that you say you have seen every other country in Europe?"

"Well," answered M———. "I have been twice to Italy, up and down, and done it as thoroughly as any man could do it. I have been—"

"Stop a wee," said I, "how have you *done* Italy? let me see, suppose we just begin in the middle, let us take Florence—no doubt you were there."

"Oh dear, yes, and such a jolly place, where one could live and love for ever! oh, yes,

> " ' Of all the fairest cities of the world,
>   None is so fair as Florence !'

"'If it were not for the heat, and having been there twice already, it would beat going to see the sun at midnight, which we shall see in Lapland, old fellow. We shall see the sun going right round the horizon, neither rising nor setting — not a bit — but going just as in the old riddle we had when we were children, 'going round and round the house, and never touching the house.' So now no more 'shirking and lurking,' but let's be off to Lapland, and if there are a few mosquitoes, we can take plenty of flea-powder to protect us; there now, I'll stand the flea-powder—a whole pound's worth," and the laugh of that excellent fellow rings in my ears still.

Here R—— joined in the conversation; he had never been to Italy, and his curiosity was raised by the enthusiastic expressions of my friend M——, in regard to Florence.

"Do tell us something about that place, where you could live and love for ever," said he.

"Well, what *can* I tell you?" replied M——. "Florence was the capital of Tuscany, and is situated on the banks of the river Arno, and it is a most delightful place. What more do you want? There is the charming Mrs. ——, and her equally charming daughter, whose house opens just as the opera closes; and once there, one never thinks of leaving till three o'clock in the morning at soonest. Then there are the Cascine, the Café Doney, and the club, and my friend G. M——y; and then the churches and the galleries, and the pietre dure, &c., &c., I did every one of them."

" Where did you go when you left Florence ?"

" To Rome, naturally."

" So all you know about Tuscany and Central Italy resolves itself into the Cascine, the Café Doney, and our friend G. M——y. Did you not even visit Siena on your way to Rome ?"

" No, for, being fond of the sea, I went to Rome by Civita Vecchia."

" When you were at Civita Vecchia, did it not come into your head to visit the birth-place of the Tarquins—Corneto? only a short drive from Civita Vecchia, and one of the most interesting places in Italy."

" I never even heard of it," said M——.

I was going to say *ex uno disce omnes,* this is how *la jeunesse doré* of the present time travel on the continent—to finish their education, by the way! but my remark would be of too sweeping a character, for there are many exceptions to be met with occasionally. Still, though travelling is multiplied a thousand-fold compared with what it used to be even only a century ago, it is doubtful, I think, if travelling is as fruitful of good results in our days as it used to be in the days of our grandfathers, when, under the guidance of a well qualified tutor, young men used to take the "grand tour" with a view to completing their education, the foundation and groundwork of which had been laid first in our public schools, and then in our great universities. Now my friend M——— was a charming fellow, well educated to a certain point, pleasant, agreeable, and good-tempered; he had travelled a good deal, and yet I may safely say he had seen nothing, and simply because he had not prepared himself for travelling with a view to thoroughly seeing the countries he intended visiting, and obtaining the information they could bestow. And how many are there that just travel in the same way! How many are there among those who yearly flood the approaches to the Eternal City who do more than lounge about the galleries, the Campo Vaccino, or the Pincian Hill! and who, if asked about the City of Veii (for instance) will simply open their eyes and say they never heard of it, where is it? Why, my good fellow, Veii was a great city, and its inhabitants among the most civilized and luxurious in the world, long before Rome was built. What! before Rome was built? he will say; and then if some mild reminiscence of the kind comes across his memory, he may, perhaps, recall some fleeting visions of Agamemnon and Mycenæ, taking it for granted that Veii, if anterior to Rome, must have been in Greece; but when informed that Veii was the rival of Rome, that its ruins were within twenty miles of the Eternal City, he will possibly get angry and think you are chaffing him. He, no doubt, may have heard of Etruria, but probably in his mind it was jumbled up with Minton's pottery; if associated with Wedgewood, it will be a point in his favour. He may probably have heard of Etruscan cities and Etruscan vases, but all his information in this line is terribly hazy ; and so he dawdles through his sojourn at Rome, goes on to Naples, perhaps to Palermo and Malta, returning to England by the P. and O. steamer, imagining that he has seen, or *done*, Italy, as he terms it.

It so happened that I had made arrangements

for another tour, and was thus unable to join my three friends in their intended expedition; but the following Winter M—— and 1 went to the continent together, we spent four months in Italy, that Italy he had so thoroughly "done" twice before! and to his amazement, he had to confess that in his previous journeys he had simply wasted his time and his money.

We visited numberless out of the way places, having made Florence our head-quarters for Central Italy, and there under the guidance of Micali's *Antichi Popoli Italiani*, we dived into the history of Italy, beginning with the misty periods synchronous with the siege of Troy, illustrating them as we went along by visits to the ancient cities and cemeteries of Etruria, and thence through those glorious Middle Ages and their unparalleled works of art, which can nowhere be so well studied as in Italy! It was a surpassing pleasure to him, no doubt, to see for the first time all those wondrous things; but it was almost as great a delight to me to witness his raptures, his astonishment, as city after city came under our examination—Fiesole, Volterra, Chiusi, Cortona. This last, especially, struck him with astonishment, a city co-eval with Ilium, and still in our days a city preserving its ancient name, while of Ilium, *periére ipsæ ruinæ*, and its very existence questioned, till the researches of the indefatigable Schliemann brought monuments to light within the last few months which have clearly identified the spot, and proved to a demonstration that Ilium really had existed, and that the siege of Troy was not simply a myth, a poet's dream!

I well remember helping him to measure the immense blocks of the ancient walls of Cortona, fitted with such wonderful exactness that the blade of a penknife can even at present be scarcely pushed in between them, and which still remain *in situ* without mortar or other cement, though probably thirty centuries have rolled on since those walls were erected by the ancestors of their present inhabitants. How I remember the interest he took in scanning from the hill which looks over the rippling water of the Trasymene Lake, pointing out the probable spot where those false-hearted Romans had rested whilst the battle was raging below, only to be overtaken, however, on the morrow by Hannibal and his victorious legions, who made them pay so dearly for their treachery.

" This is the way I like to study history, and this is the way never to forget it," said he. " I hated the very names of Tacitus and Livy, but how delightful I think them now!" and so we did *do* Italy from Agrigentum to the Alps, and from the Adriatic to the Mediterranean, and many queer out-of-the-way places we visited, and such scores of sketches we carried away; and a more delightful trip never was made before or since.

Captain Hutchinson, in his introduction to " Try Lapland," writes, " The difficulty of finding new ground for travel is increasing every year for those who, with but a limited time at their disposal, are yet tired of the beaten paths of Ramsgate or Scarborough, Switzerland or the Rhine, and pant after lands fresh and fair, of which they have never seen the photograph—where the gorgeous hotel with its elongated bills, and the pertinacious touter with his cringing greasy manners, are alike unknown."

Now to a great extent that pleasant writer is correct; but the man who rushing away from the turmoil and bustle of London life, whether he be lawyer, merchant, or physician, seeking for fresh air and scenery, but as far away as possible from those hackneyed tracks infested by the typical tourist, both English and Transatlantic, and by poor Marryat's " shilling-seeking, napkin-holding, up-and-downstairs son of a sea-cook" of an hotel waiter, need not go to the Arctic Circle to find all the above-named advantages, unless, indeed, he is bent on also seeing the sun at midnight, and his own body a prey to the mosquitoes.

Within five days of Temple Bar, or as we soon shall have to say, where Temple Bar once stood, there are as splendid countries to explore, as fine ruins to contemplate, as glorious scenery and as gorgeous costumes to admire, as the heart of man can wish for ; and if the reader will trust himself with me for a little while, excusing the many short-comings he will meet with in these pages, I will lead him over a trip I took last Summer which I think will fully repay him, though he will often have to make great allowances and deal leniently with the Author, who for the first time in his life rushes into print, just for the same reason that the stars shine above us, because he has nothing else to do! But if through publishing this little book he shall have opened up a new field of travel to those who yearly require to recruit their strength of body and of mind by a ramble in foreign lands, if he shall have added one more possible source of enjoyment to those within the reach of the many, he will consider himself amply repaid for whatever trouble he may have been put to in its compilation.

CHAPTER II.

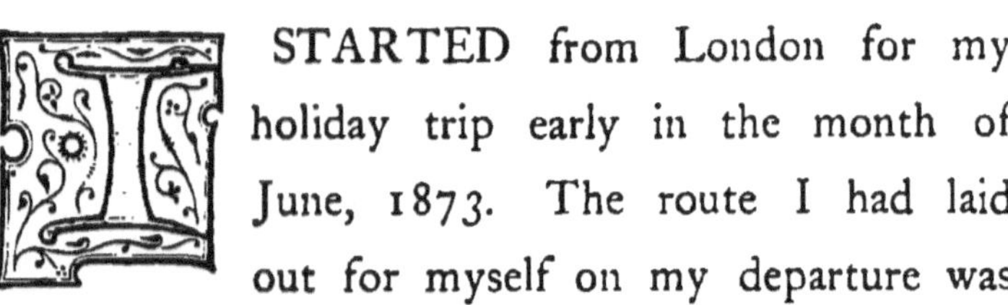

STARTED from London for my holiday trip early in the month of June, 1873. The route I had laid out for myself on my departure was not exactly that which I eventually adopted, for nothing is truer than that man proposes, but God disposes. I had intended visiting the Crimea, and then crossing over the Straits of Kertch, I meant to have rambled over the Caucasus, finishing my trip with a visit to the Monastery of Echmiadzin, at the foot of Mount Ararat.

But it was not to be; I got as far as Pesth, when the cholera, which was then very active, not to say raging in Hungary, barred my further passage down the river into the Lower Provinces of the Danube, by threatening me with a quarantine of eleven days in a dirty lazzaretto, at a temperature of at least 90° in the shade. I would have risked the cholera, but I could not face the loss of eleven days in the limited time I had at my disposal, nor could I contemplate at all the horrors of an Oriental lazzaretto. All my plans were therefore upset; still the result was eventually satisfactory, as I think I shall be able to prove in the following pages.

After leaving London, I made straight for Vienna, by Brussels and Cologne, where I remained only a few hours, during which I visited for the twentieth time and more that exquisite specimen of ecclesiastical structure, its unrivalled Cathedral; every time I see it I admire it more and more, I think there are none to equal it, while most certainly none surpass it.

St. Peter's at Rome is a magnificent building, astonishes one by its size and its rich adornments, but it fails to impress one from a religious point of view. It might be a church, or it might be a grand reception room, a *salle des ambassadeurs,* or a colossal ball-room—whereas the Cathedral of Cologne is a church, a place of worship, and nothing else. I suppose there is something in the pure Gothic architecture conducive to this impression. There is but one other church I know of in the world which has the same solemn awe-producing effect, perhaps in a greater degree even than the Cathedral of Cologne, and that is Santa Maria del Fiore, the Cathedral of Florence. I have been hundreds of times in that grand old edifice, but never without feeling an overwhelming sense of solemnity and awe. It was not only the low murmuring notes of the organ sounding the responses at eve to the plaintive litanies of the Virgin, nor the deep tones of the full accompaniment to the *Miserere mei Deus* in the Passion Week, which produced it, for I was perhaps oftener there when all was silent, than during festive times, as I have always had the greatest objection to going into Catholic churches during service, gaping about and sight-seeing, to the evident annoyance and discomfort of the worshippers—a habit which, I regret to say, many of our country people too often indulge in, greatly to our detriment, especially in the less frequented places of the continent, where the people have come to regard us as heathens, and constantly to say of us, "Non sanno meglio, non sono Cristiani."

It was something more than all this which ever filled me with a feeling of intense devotion when I entered that grand old building. The severe simplicity of the structure, with no tawdry ornamentation to obtrude itself and take off the attention, may have played an important part in giving birth to solemn thoughts, together with the height and size of the three enormous pilasters which alone support the roof—the lofty arches, the vast depth and gloom of the aisles, the intensity of the shade, the deep silence made still more impressive by an occasional foot-fall—all would combine to proclaim this a house of prayer, and nothing else; a Temple in the fullest and most unequivocal sense of the word, offering to the old and the broken-spirited, to the infirm and to all who sought it in prayer, an assurance of tranquillity, consolation, and peace!

Having enjoyed my oft-repeated visit, and purchased a large supply of Eau de Cologne from the Farina *gegenüber dem Julichs Platz*, (and don't you believe that the others make it near as good), I got in the train for Munich and for Vienna.

I think I see a smile, slightly perhaps savouring of a sneer, from some of my readers of the masculine gender, at my purchase of a large supply of Eau de Cologne; but just let them hold hard, till they shall have endured the trials of hot winds and dusty roads in the daytime, stuffy cabins and the ordinary accompaniment of flea invasions and other entomological attacks in the night-time; and then if they have the luck to have any of it with them, they will discover the use of Eau de Cologne in allaying pain and irritation.

Travellers in all Eastern countries should have with them a supply of good Eau de Cologne, not for scenting their pocket-handkerchiefs only, but principally as a remedy. Some people suffer more, some suffer less from insect attacks; but I have seen a man, a strong, stout, brawny Britisher, set nearly wild by flea-bites, and I shall never forget his appearance, as he stood before me one morning, after passing a restless night in a very wild region in the South of Europe, like a patient with small-pox, and scratching away at himself for bare life. I am sure he would have been in a high fever that night, had I not bathed him with a mixture of equal parts of Eau de Cologne, laurel water, and sal-volatile. So don't forget it, kind reader, if ever in your travels you are likely to be in countries infested with insect tribes; whatever their nature may be, whether the mosquito which flieth, the flea which hoppeth, or t'other thing which crawleth, my nostrum will be found a sovereign remedy against them all.

Although the Vienna Exhibition was fully open, and that numbers were flocking from all parts to that most charming capital, which has so justly acquired the epithet of "le Paradis des Hommes," I was fortunate in having but one companion in the train all the way, and thus we both were enabled to extend our limbs and sleep as comfortably as in our beds. It is wonderful the amount of comfort one can obtain through life by the judicious distribution of a few cigars accompanied by a little silver!

At Vienna, I went—as I always do—to the Archduke Charles' Hotel; a little old-fashioned, perhaps, but unquestionably the best hotel in Vienna, and where the cooking is always undeniable. During my short stay, I went every day to the Universal Exhibition—the world's fair! but don't be afraid that I mean to weary you by dragging you with me through those confusing avenues of "all sorts," where nothing that was wanted could be found, and everything we wanted not was sure to be everlastingly obtruding itself before our eyes.

I confess that the Vienna Exhibition disappointed me; whereas the Paris one of 1867 left me nothing to desire; and all owing to the want of order and system in the one instance—while in the other, the arrangement was so perfect that there was not the smallest difficulty in getting at anything one wanted to find out.

But if the exhibitional department was less perfect in its arrangement at Vienna than at Paris, the gardens and the outside accessories were far more beautiful at the former than the latter; while Strauss's delightful band always afforded an hour's luxurious enjoyment in the cool of the afternoon, till the fearful braying of the steam trumpet, (they called it a Telephone, I think) drove one out into the Prater. Then the restaurants and cafés of the different Nationalities were so well got up and so picturesquely scattered about the Gardens, as were also the several buildings characteristic of the different Nations, and among which was pre-eminent for elegance of form, design, and execution, the kiosk of the Pasha of Egypt.

And then the Viennese ladies! I know I should have mentioned them the first, I confess it; *confiteor, mea culpa, mea maxima culpa,* but, gentle reader, it was from sheer diffidence! I did not know how to approach the subject, I felt myself totally incompetent, and indeed I do so now! To say that at Vienna there are more lovely women to be seen than in any other city in Europe, is not saying one half. There are loads of pretty women to be seen in Dublin of a fine Sunday afternoon, especially among the middle and lower classes; but at Vienna they are not only lovely, but terribly attractive, and winning, and seductive; there are none like them anywhere else!

In the fine arts department there were many beautiful things to be seen; but as I promised not to drag the reader round the World's Fair, I shall keep my word, and shall only call his attention to two statues which greatly attracted me, one was a bronze figure of a Hindoo charming a cobra, the other a Negro running away, both figures perfectly alive!

I went twice to the opera, once to hear Meyerbeer's "Africaine," which disappointed me; and once to see a grand ballet, I think it was called "Eleonora," which did not. I had not been for several years at Vienna, and had, therefore, not seen the new Opera House. I was greatly struck with its size and beauty; it is unquestionably the finest theatre in Europe, and the arrangements are perfect. But Vienna is now undergoing such a process of transformation, and to such an extent, that in a few years those who knew it ten or twelve years ago will be utterly unable to recognise it. Even now it is one of the finest capitals in Europe, but at the rate it is progressing, it bids fair to surpass in a short time every other city, when the Viennese will really be able to give utterance with truth to their old saying, "Gibt nur eine Kaiserstadt, gibt nur ein Wien !"

After a very delightful week in Vienna, which seemed indeed far too short a time to bestow upon the most enjoyable capital in Europe, I took my passage in a steamer to Pesth, starting at six a.m., and arriving at my destination at about the same hour in the evening. The steamer was a very fine one, the accommodation excellent, the cuisine not good, but then I had been terribly spoilt at the Erz-Herzog Karl; probably had I been at a worse hotel, I would not have found so much fault with the cookery on board the steamer. The company on board was worse than the cookery—in all my rambles I don't think I ever met so unprepossessing a lot.

The large steamers that navigate the Danube don't come up to Vienna, but lie off the Island of Lobau, to which passengers are carried in a smaller steamer. The morning I started was drizzling and chilly in the extreme, in marked contrast with the weather of the previous week, which had been intensely hot; and when I sat down on the deck of the little steamer which was to take me down a branch of the Danube to the main steamer, I was glad to avail myself of my top-coat and rugs. In a short time we reached the larger vessel, and, having all got on board, we started at a good round speed.

From Vienna to Gran, the Danube is uninterest-ing so far as scenery is concerned. Its enormous volume of muddy water, wider than the Thames at Westminster, though still upwards of nine hundred miles from its entrance into the Black Sea, flows through a vast flat country; an interminable front of sallows and alders on the one side, and an interminable plain on the other, dotted all over with countless herds of white cattle with long black horns like the Tuscan oxen, and endless troops of horses; and as I gazed on the mighty flood of turbid waters, the old Italian nursery rhyme came back to my memory.

> " Tre Ombroni fanno un Arno,
> Tre Arni fanno un Tevere,
> Tre Tevere fanno un Pò,
> E tre Pò di Lombardia
> Fanno un Danubio di Turchia."

We passed by Pressburg where the two sides of the river are united by a bridge of boats. We only remained a short time and I had no opportunity of going ashore, so that I could form but a very inaccurate opinion of the place; it seemed to me from its outward look as not now prosperous, but had quite the appearance of having seen better days.

After a time we came to Komorn, the cele-

brated fortress; if I had not been told, "There is
Komorn," I might almost have passed it without
observing it, so protected from sight are its bastions
by the immense earthworks in front of them. Still
down we steamed, and still the same country
right and left met our view, till we came to Gran,
the seat of the Prince-Primate of Hungary,
perhaps one of the wealthiest prelates in the world,
possessing no less an income than £90,000
per annum.

Here the scenery began to improve; the Cathedral
of Gran, though in itself unclassical, and one that
in any other place might be passed by unnoticed,
yet served to relieve the monotony of the view.
The river, which up to this had flowed through
boundless plains, became suddenly contracted, and
consequently swifter as the high lands approached
the edge of it; and now with every revolu-
tion of the paddles the scenery improved, till
on reaching Vissegrad it became absolutely
lovely. Instead of the interminable plains, we now
had precipitous mountains on either side, some
clad with forest down to the water's edge, some
bare, ragged, and rocky, but all lovely, quite

equal to the finest parts of the Rhine, not even lacking a Drachenfels in the beautiful ruins of the ancient castellated palace of the Kings of Hungary, the favourite retreat of the learned Matthias Corvinus.

Nature has done everything to beautify this favoured spot, but man, as is too often the case, has done his best to mar it. At the foot of the cliff, the top of which is crowned by the ancient residence of the Kings of Hungary, on a beautifully wooded spot between the mountain and the rushing Danube, some enterprising German has erected, *horribile visu*, three villa residences, in the correct suburban style, a few yards distant from one another. Regardless of expense, everything about them, including themselves, is radiant with white-wash, except where green paint asserts its place. At first I thought it must be an hotel or pension, with two *succursales;* but no, the skipper assured me they were country houses, and seemed astonished when I said the man that built them deserved to be hanged in front of them; he could not comprehend me, he thought them lovely!

Often during my subsequent travels I thought

of that lovely country between Gran and Vissegrad;
such exquisite scenery, so diversified; such a
combination of rolling pastures, of glorious hills
clad with forests, backed by rugged mountains,
with that grand old Danube rushing through the
midst; such shooting and fishing, all in a
compact locality, and only four hours by rail from
Vienna; such a spot for a country residence
could scarcely be equalled, and certainly not
surpassed. If it were within ten hours of
London, what a fabulous price it would command! but here no one seems to have
placed any value on it since the days of Matthias
Corvinus.

After going through this gorge, the Danube
spreads itself out again, and the scenery becomes
tame and uninteresting, and continues so till one
reaches Pesth, where I arrived somewhat later
than I expected.

CHAPTER III.

I DROVE to the Hotel Ungaria, to which I had been recommended, and where a most comfortable apartment and an equally good dinner gave me an *avant-goût* of a comfortable night's rest, in which I was no wise disappointed; and I can safely recommend the Ungaria as one of the finest and most comfortable hotels in Europe, without at the same

time being extravagant in its charges. The only
drawback I found was with the person of the porter,
a most respectable man no doubt, but he could
not speak either French or English ; and I had
to carry on all my consultations respecting my
intended future progress with the hall-porter of
the " Königin von England" hotel, close by.
If that man could only be installed at the Ungaria,
that hotel would be as near perfection as
possible.

The windows of my bedroom at the Ungaria
opened out on a balcony which gave me a
splendid view of the "blue Danube," which, however, I never saw of any other shade but mud
colour. Across the river, and just opposite, I
could see the ancient city of Buda, with the royal
residence in front, and a little to the left, on
the top of the hill, the celebrated fortress which
played so important a part during the last
Hungarian civil war. A little to my right was
the grand suspension bridge, guarded at each
end by two colossal couchant lions, about which
the following improbable anecdote was related to
me.

The artist who executed them forgot to put tongues into their mouths, to loll out in proper heraldic fashion, and when the defect was pointed out to him as the lions were uncovered, he took it so to heart that he at once put an end to himself by plunging headlong into the river! Now when "le grand Vatel" committed suicide, because the turbot did not arrive in time for the dinner of the Most Christian King, there was some show of reason in the act, Vatel's credit was in some degree pledged to that dinner; but not one man ·in ten thousand would have noticed whether these lions had tongues or not.

Pesth seems, like Vienna, to be undergoing a process of rebuilding, and that on a scale of considerable magnificence. I was told that its commerce was daily increasing, and, certainly, to judge from the immense number of vessels moored in the river, the ceaseless passing up and down of immense steamers, the piles of merchandize, and the constant bustle on the quays, a very considerable amount of business must be done there. The grand suspension

bridge which spans the Danube being found
insufficient for the increasing traffic, a new one
is in process of construction, to be built of
iron on piers, and not a suspension bridge. It
is to cost an immense sum, and will require
to be well protected against the action of the
ice on the one hand, while on the other it
may become the source of considerable danger
to the low land in its neighbourhood by
arresting the free passage downwards of the
ice, if not well looked after. I went to see
the works at the central pier, and remained there
some time watching the men at the bottom of
the immense caisson out of which a donkey
engine was incessantly pumping water; outside it,
the river was running like a mill race at not
less than eight miles an hour, and I was
assured that the depth at that spot was fully forty
feet.

After visiting the works at the new bridge,
I went to St. Marguerite's Island, on which
is a park beautifully laid out, and which forms
one of the favourite promenades of the pleasure-
loving inhabitants of Pesth. As it can only

be approached by boat, it is frequented only by pedestrians; but in order to cater for all tastes and gratify those who enjoy a jaunt, there is a tramway running the whole length of the island. There are also some capital restaurants, and several bands play every evening in fine weather.

There is another park on *terra firma*, an imitation of the Prater at Vienna, but it is small and shabby. There were a good many people strolling about it when I went, but I did not see even one middling-good turn-out, and though one constantly hears of the beautiful horses and rare horsemanship of the Hungarians, I was doomed to be disappointed in both cases.

Crossing over the suspension bridge one gets into the old town of Buda or Ofen, in which are situated the Royal residence, the Government offices, and some of the palaces of the native magnates.

There is a fine street by which one can drive to the upper part of the town, which is considerably above the level of the Danube; but for pedestrians there is an easy, cheap, and quick method of getting to the summit, by means of a small counterpoised railway, which carries one up and down very rapidly at an exceedingly moderate rate. There is a fine view from the top, and several fine old palaces, but the most interesting thing in the town of Buda is the old Roman bath erected over some sulphurous springs, celebrated for the cures they perform. It is in exactly the same condition as in the days of ancient Rome, and consists of a large vaulted apartment lit by a circular opening in the centre of the cupola, and containing a large hexagonal piscina with an ambulatory all round. None bathe there save the lower classes—men, women, and children promiscuously; in the immediate neighbourhood, however, there are some very well appointed baths which are considerably patronized, and bear a high reputation for the cure of skin disease.

From all I could collect during the brief stay I made at Pesth, Hungary in general must be in a very progressive condition; and from the numbers of agricultural machines and implements, all of English construction, which I saw everywhere stacked upon the quays, not only at Pesth but at many other stations on the Danube, including large numbers of steam-thrashing and winnowing machines, a vigorous attempt is evidently being made to exploit the unbounded fertility of perhaps the richest soil in Europe. Land, however, is still cheap in Hungary, probably in consequence of the extreme love of pleasure of its inhabitants, who preferring to spend their days in the society of Vienna, Paris, or Pesth, draw exorbitantly on their revenues, till at last compelled to sell their lands in order to meet their engagements. Nice estates within twenty miles of Pesth, with good substantial dwelling-houses, and all the necessary offices for farming, with varied soil, vineyard, pasture, tillage, and forest, can be had sufficiently cheap to ensure a clear return of five per cent, free of taxes, for the capital laid out on them! A vast number of the agricultural community in Hungary are Jews, and it is perhaps the only country in Europe where we find the children of Israel as tillers of the soil; and I was assured by many in Pesth that they make by far the most satisfactory tenants—though naturally they require looking after occasionally, as well as their *soi-disant* Christian brethren.

When one reflects on the countless acres of the richest land in creation, which to a great extent are still unoccupied and uncultivated in the eastern and south-eastern regions of Europe, one cannot help regretting that some of our surplus population do not try a venture in those countries. I am thinking principally of that most unfortunate and ill-used portion of society belonging to the upper classes, and which, from circumstances beyond its control, is suffering from positive want in its struggles to keep up a respectability as necessary for its existence as the very air it breathes. The labourer, the artisan, the skilled workman are well off at the present time in our country ; wages are very high and the friendly societies, to one of which almost every workman belongs, provide for them amply in cases of sickness, and in some cases even contribute something to the family when the illness terminates in death—not to mention the numerous hospitals and asylums, all open to the labouring classes, but which are all virtually closed to those I am now speaking of.

The working classes, with few exceptions, are all well off at present, and require none of our sympathy except when in affliction, when the richest and poorest come to the same level. They can afford to supply all their wants out of their wages, and lay out *one fifth*, and in many cases *one fourth*, and even *one third* (I am assured by good authorities) in drink, for the gratification of the only pleasure which they are capable of enjoying; for proof of which the police reports throughout the country will bear ample evidence.

But I will tell who really deserve all our sympathy and all our aid, the junior branches of our upper ten thousand—the families of officers, poor clergymen, poor lawyers, &c., &c., all struggling for dear life against difficulties of every kind; those are the classes who claim the greatest share of our sympathy, and to whom the regions above mentioned offer advantages unequalled any where else.

I remember when the Canterbury settlement

was established in New Zealand, it was intended
in a great measure to provide for the classes I
have alluded to above; but the distance was too
great, the mere cost of going out was a most
serious drawback, at the very least *ten times* the
amount required to land one bag and baggage in the
centre of Hungary, or better still in Servia, among
some of the most beautiful scenery in the world,
the richest soil, the best climate, and the finest
fishing and shooting that could be desired, where
game laws and river preserves and licences are
still utterly unknown.

I hate croaking; still, if one hears rumbling
noises underground for any space of time, one
is justified in apprehending an earthquake. For
several years I have been hearing these subterranean noises, and year after year they have
become more and more threatening, and the
earthquake must come at last. But as a volcanic
eruption, acting as a safety valve, often saves a
country from the effects of a physical earthquake, so the timely exodus of an excessive
population may save a country from a moral
one.

By the very nature of my profession, I have innumerable times been willingly or unwillingly let into the secrets of the private affairs of scores of families; and I have watched with perfect dismay the misery, the poverty, the utter wretchedness that were screened from the eyes of the world by the decent exterior which was kept up in order to preserve appearances.

If with Asmodeus we could but lift up the roofs of a few thousands of houses in these prosperous islands and see the difficulties, the make-shifts, and the make-believes which are resorted to, and that in many cases where one would least expect them, it would make our very hearts bleed at all the anxiety, all the wretchedness, all the scalding tears which would be disclosed—all brought about by that great delusion " keeping up appearances." Well, all this living under false pretences, which is the distinguishing characteristic and the great evil, the real " social evil " of the present time cannot go on for ever. It is an evil of long standing, no doubt, but it has gone on increasing from year to year, like a falling avalanche, with constantly increasing velocity.

The earthquake must come at last, if not averted by an emigration *en masse* of those educated classes to which I have alluded above; and the best, finest, healthiest, most fertile, and most accessible country, outside the British dominions, I hold to be, roughly speaking, that tract of Southern Europe bounded on the North by the Saave, on the South by the Bosphorus, on the East by the Danube, and on the West by the Adriatic.

"But, my dear Sir," I think I hear some reader say, "that is Turkey in Europe!" No doubt it is, but the Turks won't be there for ever, their time is nearly run out; the period of their wretched misrule over the Christian populations of Europe is nearly accomplished, and I still hope to live long enough to see those barbarous hordes recrossing the Bosphorus into Asia Minor, on their way back to the Steppes of Khiva and Bokhara, from whence they originally emigrated. They have ever shown themselves irreclaimable barbarians throughout. Look at the present condition of European Turkey, after centuries of Ottoman dominion; contrast it with the nascent state of Roumania, which only quite lately succeeded in shaking off its Moslem chains. Let us look at both countries, as they present themselves opposite to each other on the banks of the Danube. On the left bank of that river we have Giurgevo in Roumania, the port of Bukharest, where, notwithstanding centuries of slavery and misgovernment, the natives, now under the government of an enlightened Christian Prince, are all activity and progress—while on the right bank at Rustchuk, just opposite, in dark contrast to the Christian, who is trying to turn to account all the advantages of his country, the indolent, un-civilized Turk is still lazily dozing away, leaning against his ancient painted and bedizened araba, drawn by a pair of patient oxen, waiting for the chance of some solitary, silent traveller !

A new era is dawning, however, over these south-eastern regions, but much of their prosperity and future happiness may depend on the model they will propose for themselves in their efforts at civilization; whether the brilliant glitter of Parisian veneering and varnish, or the less attrac-

tive, but more solid advantages of British institutions.   A great future is before the Danubian
Principalities, may they use their opportunities with
wisdom, and may they prosper !

CHAPTER IV.

THAT odious and useless mediæval institution, the quarantine, having barred my passage into the Lower Provinces of the Danube, I determined to go to Trieste, then proceed by sea to Constantinople, and thence to the Caucasus, but it was written differently in the book of Fate!

The line to Trieste was full of interest; during the first portion of the journey I passed quite close to Lake Balaton, celebrated for its fish, and then after traversing some wonderfully rich plains, dotted here and there with patches of forest, and covered with herds of cattle, horses, and geese, which are kept here in vast numbers for the sake of their feathers, arrived at Steinbrück at one p.m., where I dined. Here, at the junction of the Saane and the Saave, the scenery became truly magnificent; we had been for some time following the banks of the Saane, and the mountains had been getting closer and higher with every mile we made, till at last they actually came down to the river, allowing a bare passage to the railway which followed its every bend.

Having finished our mid-day meal at Steinbrück—where the Pesth line joins on to that miracle of engineering, the celebrated railway between Vienna and Trieste—we resumed our journey, the scenery retaining its grand features, till having topped the Sömmering, we came on to the desert Karst and got our first peep of the salt water—the glorious Adriatic. Nothing could exceed the wild grandeur of the country on both sides of the railway, as the engines (for we had two of them) slowly panted up those steep inclines, winding in and out through the gorges of the Sömmering, now plunging into a tunnel to traverse the heart of a mountain, and now crossing a viaduct between two cliffs, over a precipice hundreds of feet in depth. Once at the top, our pace increased considerably, and by eight o'clock I found myself comfortably installed at my hotel at Trieste, on the evening of the 29th of June.

After a most refreshing night, I descended the next morning to the café on the ground floor of the hotel, and then heard for the first time of the severe shocks of earthquake at Belluno and its neighbourhood, which had been felt even in Trieste. Several lives had been lost, and one church nearly shaken to the ground.

After breakfast I went to pay my respects to our excellent consul, Captain Burton, and then hearing that the Austrian ironclad " Lissa " was outside the harbour, I took a boat and went to have a look at her. She is a fine vessel with a long projecting prow, and looks well in the water. Having sent up my card, I was received and shown over the ship by Lieutenant Count Petruski, who was most kind in pointing out every thing of interest connected with it. I think he said she mounted 12 rifled fifteen-ton guns of our Woolwich Infant type, and was furnished with a galvanic apparatus, by means of which the captain could fire a whole broadside at a time. Although she was only in after a cruise, and consequently not in the best of trim for exhibition, I was much gratified by all I saw. The men were a very fine set of fellows, the state cabins and officers' cabins particularly neat and nice, and should these lines ever fall beneath the eye of Count Petruski or any of his brother officers on board the " Lissa" I beg them all to receive my warm thanks for their kindness to me that day. I spent a couple of very pleasant hours on board, and as Count Petruski spoke excellent English, it made our interview all the more agreeable.*

* Since writing the above I have obtained the following authentic description of this ship. The " Lissa" ironclad was built at Trieste.

Trieste is anything but an interesting place ; though a couple of days may be spent pleasantly enough visiting the neighbourhood, especially if one has the advantage of the acquaintance and company of our consul, Captain R. Burton ; the Burton of Harar, of Mecca, and of Medina ; the *facile princeps* of modern travellers and pleasant companions.

Why is Captain Burton kept at Trieste ? It is not a difficult post, nor one requiring a man with exceptional qualifications ; and it does seem a misapplication if not a waste of *force* to keep a man like Burton at Trieste, when he could be of so much greater use elsewhere. The thorough and intimate knowledge that he possesses of

She is a full-rigged casemated ironclad of 5950 tons, 320 feet long, 60 feet beam, and drawing 28 feet of water. Armoured with 6-inch Austrian plates, the armament consisting of ten 9-inch breech-loading Krupp guns in her maindeck casemate, and two 9-inch breech-loading Krupp guns on turn-tables in semi-circular overhanging casemates on the open deck, the guns being protected from above by a sort of central hurricane deck. The "Lissa" steams at the rate of twelve knots, and carries coals for 420 hours ; among other improvements she has a powerful electric light placed on the bridge, and gimballed, so as to allow it to be thrown in any direction.

Oriental character, his perfect mastery of Arabic, together with the knowledge he has of Persian and scores of other languages, not to mention the experience he has acquired of Oriental affairs, customs and idiosyncrasies, all go to point him out emphatically as the right man in the wrong place at Trieste. I spent some very pleasant hours in his company during my short stay in that city, and shall never forget the kindness I experienced both from him and la bella Contessa, his most charming and accomplished lady. ·

Thus far, my observations have been of a strictly selfish nature. I know Captain Burton's capabilities, I feel that he is utterly thrown away where he is, and I want a *quid pro quo* for my money—consequently I want to see him in some post where his talents and exceptional qualifications may be of some profit to me. The reader will perceive that I am strictly selfish and utilitarian, and that in writing as above I have not been led away by sentimentality in any shape. Had I been in the opposite vein, I could have said, I met at Trieste Captain R. T. Burton, who undoubtedly is the greatest of *living* travellers, and also second to none in that great phalanx of explorers, who from time to time have devoted their lives to carrying civilization to the most remote corners of the earth. He opened up Eastern Africa, and most probably discovered in Lake Tanganyika the mysterious sources of the Nile. He directly opened up the path and led the way which was subsequently trodden by Speke, Grant, Stanley, Cameron, and others; indirectly he pointed out the way to Baker, Schweinfurth and Gordon. To Richard Burton then is due the discovery of this *New Africa*, this great Lake Region, so fertile and so rich in the centre of a continent which fifty years ago was believed to be one vast uninhabitable desert. What has been his reward? He has been made consul at Trieste. Here is an inducement to our ardent British youth! I hear there is some talk of making him a K.C.B.; for myself, I wouldn't give a roll of ginger-bread for the distinction; however, let him have it by all means, but let us see him also removed to some more useful sphere of action where his exceptional talents and his great knowedge of Oriental languages may be of service to us. Let him be sent to Africa again—to Morocco for instance—at the first vacancy.

Having still to wait a couple of days for the departure of the steamer which was to take me on my trip down the coast of Dalmatia, I employed my time in paying a flying visit to San Canziano, where a good-sized river, after meandering down a deep ravine like any other Christian stream, suddenly plunges into the bowels of the earth, and after a mysterious course of many miles, re-appears again at the surface under a different name, previous to losing itself in the Adriatic.

The little hamlet of San Canziano is about twenty miles from Trieste, it consists of a very small and meanly built church, with a good campanile however, with two sweetly-toned bells—why is it that ours are always so unmusical and woody?— a small wretched Presbytery, a roadside pot-house where nothing could be got for love or money, and half a dozen dilapidated houses. The drive however, was very pleasant, for the weather was warm and at the same time cloudy, so that we were never inconvenienced by the sun. The road, on leaving Trieste, goes by easy windings over a mountain clothed with oak, so beautifully kept, that it gives the idea of driving through some private park. On reaching the top we came into the open, and had a glorious view of the Styrian mountains on the one side, and the Adriatic on the other. After driving for a short time on the level, we again commenced ascending and soon got into the "Karst," as it is called; a wild barren tract where little or nothing appears to grow, and where rocks and stones seem to have rained down from heaven, not unlike some other spots I visited subsequently in Dalmatia, and notably in Montenegro. But this bleak and barren spot owes its absolute desolation, not so much to the rocky nature of its soil, as to the Bora, a north-east wind, which often sweeps across it with the force of a West Indian hurricane.

In many places on the road, traverses of immensely thick stone walls had been erected for protection against the fury of the wind, but notwithstanding all, the Karst is sometimes impassable when the Bora blows in real earnest, and heavy-laden waggons which have tried to cross it at such times, have been turned over and over like " leaves in Autumn weather." After travelling for some short time along this elevated plateau, we again began to descend, and soon reached our destination, where, having eaten the lunch I had brought with me, I started on foot, under the guidance of a native who could speak nothing but Styrian, to seek the mysterious river.

In less than half an hour's walk, I found myself on a grass-covered plateau of some miles in extent, fringed in the distance by lofty hills, dotted with clumps of fir trees, and after a few minutes more walking in an easterly direction, I suddenly came on a perpendicular precipice, upwards of five hundred feet in depth, which completely barred my further progress. The cliff on which I stood rose in a narrow valley, or glen, or cleft, as if the crust of the earth had cracked here for a few miles. This cleft, nearly of uniform depth, was not of uniform width; in some places it was so narrow that the smooth river which glided through it completely filled it from side to side, while in other places a sufficient strip of soil remained between the river and the cliff to admit of some amount of cultivation, and here and there a cottage.

This strange cleft, or valley, or crack in the plateau through which the river flows is of a most irregular outline, going zig-zag, in and out, just like the cracks one sees in a dried up pond at the end of a hot Summer in England. I was standing where this precipitous crack barred the way, by running exactly at right angles across the path, and here right under me at a depth of about five hundred feet, the river which could be seen coursing from a considerable distance at the bottom of the cleft, suddenly leapt into a cavern and disappeared beneath my feet.

Having made a rapid sketch of this extraordinary landscape—or, more correctly speaking, having tried to convey on paper some faint idea of what the place was like—I again followed the guide, who now, turning his back on the precipice, led me in a westerly direction, and brought me in a few minutes to the brink of a fearful-looking circular chasm, about fifty yards in diameter, with precipitous rocky sides, and from the bottom of which could be heard the distant roar of the river rushing among the rocks. The guide threw some large stones down this yawning gulph, disturbing some thousands of rock-pigeons who build their nests in the nooks and crannies of the rocks, and having timed the fall of one of these stones by listening for its splash in the subterranean river, I noted about seven seconds as the time it took in falling.

I now accompanied the guide through the little hamlet of San Canziano, and still going westward came just beyond the village on another chasm, of oblong form, about six hundred yards one way, and three hundred and fifty yards the other way, while in depth it was no more than about fifty yards. It looked to me as if this opening had been made by the subsidence or falling-in of the roof of some cavern, of which the limestone rock of these mountains, as well in Styria as in Dalmatia is so full. The sides of this depression were not precipitous except in some places, and an easy descent led me to the bottom, across which stretched from side to side a fantastic ridge of rock pierced by a natural arch about the middle, and under which an opening in the rock gave entrance to another cavern, through which anyone desirous of exploring it could without much difficulty, but at the cost of some fatigue and the risk of some falls, descend by a series of about six hundred high and slippery ledges of rock to where again the river makes its appearance after its subterranean course.

As the day was pretty well advanced, and as the weather, which had been cloudy all the morning seemed now to be threatening rain, I thought it wisest not to venture on going further, although the guide had provided himself with candles for the descent. So I scrambled up the sides of the chasm, and was making for the roadside inn where the carriage was waiting for me, when the storm-clouds, which had been gathering thicker and thicker for some time, broke out at last into such a deluge of rain, accompanied by thunder and lightning, that I was glad to take refuge under the archway of the belfry of San Canziano, and from thence into the church itself, the door of which was opened for me by a queer little old dried-up chip of a sexton.

I am sure he said to me, " Pray take shelter in here from the rain," though as he spoke Styrian I could not understand a word, but his looks and gestures were as eloquent as words. Having walked into the little church, first taking off my hat, the little sexton became quite eloquent, and pointed out with evident satisfaction to every part of the chapel, which was poor and desolate in the extreme. Four white-washed walls, a wretched altar piece of wood painted in a few gaudy colours, and a crimson damask baldachino in tatters, which, stowed away in a corner, served to shelter the " Santissimo" when carried about in procession, two or three benches, a confessional box, and a lighted lamp hanging in front of the altar, constituted *toute la baraque!* but the poor little old man seemed delighted with himself and everything around him, and kept repeating in a shrill voice the only Italian word he apparently possessed " *Bella*," " *Bella*," to which I responded as in duty bound, " *molto bella*," and I trust I may be forgiven the cram; for I never told a bigger one in all my life!

The floor of this little church was formed of large flag-stones, in some of which iron rings were inserted, while in others there only remained the marks of where rings had formerly been ; some had inscriptions, and I should have been interested in hearing something of the ancient tenants of these graves, but here the sexton and I came completely to a dead lock. "*Bella*" could serve my friend no longer, still he understood perfectly what I required, so when he sat down on a bench, pointing to me to do the same, I complied at once, and all the more willingly as the rain was still coming down in torrents.

The old fellow then commenced, and, pointing with his skinny finger to the central slab, entered at once into what, I presume, must have been a full, true, and complete history of the tenants of that grave, descanting probably on their virtues, and dealing gently with their faults; but alas ! I could not understand one word. At last, I suppose the same thought must have struck "Old Mortality," for he suddenly stopped and bursting into a shrill, unearthly, and most discordant laugh, pointed to the sky which was now clearing, and held out his palsied hand, when I discovered he knew another word, not Slave, nor Italian, but this time German, "*Geschenk!*" I gave him the only bit of silver I possessed, an English sixpence, and left him seemingly contented.

The clouds had all melted away, and the sun shone brilliantly when I left the little roadside tavern of San Canziano to return to Trieste; but, as I wanted to visit a stud-park which the Emperor of Austria keeps in this part of his dominions, we took another route on my return journey. The country we now drove through was prettier than what we had traversed in the morning, and the road passed through some fine oak woods, which constantly prompted one to look out for a mansion, the country appeared so park-like—but in vain.

After a drive of an hour or so we came to the stud-farm, a collection of large buildings, consisting of several dwelling-houses, a spacious riding-house for exercising the horses in severe weather, three large stables intended to accommodate three hundred mares, and one lofty vaulted stable fitted with nice large loose boxes in which were kept the sires. The mares were all out at grass together with their foals, so that I did not see them, as I should have had to drive some miles in a different direction, and turn my back on Trieste in order to visit them. The sires I did see, but as they were not led out I could not form as accurate an opinion of them as I should have wished. They seemed, however, small, and not exactly the style of horse we would select in this country with a view to supplying our cavalry. The loose-boxes were commodious and the stable was well-ventilated; the weather being extremely hot the windows were closed with *tatties*, which served the double purpose of keeping away the flies, which always seek the light, and keeping the stable cool. The stable was fairly clean, but the grooming did not come up to our ideas. On the whole I was disappointed, and as for the produce, I should think that nothing but the very lightest of light cavalry horses could be expected from them.

We returned to Trieste by nine o'clock, coming

by the old post-road from Vienna, and passing by that wonderful quarry of limestone slabs, perhaps the largest in the world.

CHAPTER V.

N the 2nd of July I was up betimes. I had taken my place for Zara on board the 'San Carlo,' a small coasting steamer which trades down the Dalmatian side of the Adriatic, going in and out among that archi- pelago of islands which fringe the coast of Dalmatia from the mouth of the Guarnero to the entrance of the Gulf of Cattaro. It was a small, slow, and dirty little steamer, but it stopped

everywhere going on its way, and that was just what I wanted.

Small as the vessel was, we had plenty of passengers, and a strange lot they were. We had two Capuchin monks going to Ragusa, one of them a most interesting man of whom I shall have more to say by and by; his lay brother, a simple, ignorant monk, and no more. We had a tall, handsome Dalmatian from Spalato, returning home to end his days in opulence and comfort after spending twenty years in India, where he had accumulated an independence which in Dalmatia will be considered a large fortune. He spoke English remarkably well. Being struck by his hale and robust looks, I asked him how he had managed to preserve his health so well after residing for twenty years in India. " Many of them," added he, " in unhealthy localities." "Simply by not drinking," he answered. "I don't mean to say that I was a water-drinker—not at all, for I believe that water-drinking is nearly as bad as spirit-drinking, and indeed I think I have observed that those who were 'teatotallers' died even sooner than drunkards. But I never drank anything before breakfast, I drank nothing but good, full-bodied claret, and I never took more than two bottles of it a day, and seldom so much ; I smoked, but always in moderation, and I never had a day's illness during those twenty years. India is not a bad climate, it is the reckless habits of Europeans that make it apparently so."

We had two other Dalmatians from Sebenico, who also were returning home after residing many years abroad. These two had been in Australia ; one had been a digger, and seemed the reverse of well-off; the other had kept a store at some gold-diggings, and had apparently made plenty of money. Both spoke English well, and the last one brought with him from Australia an Irish wife, who had emigrated to the Antipodes all the way from Lurgan. She was a fine comely young woman of about twenty-six, and was overjoyed at finding I knew her native place. In the afternoon I made some tea in my portable kitchen, and gave her a cup of it with some preserved milk, which she declared the most delicious thing she had tasted for many a long day.

The rest of our passengers consisted of country

people returning to their homes along the coast of Istria and Dalmatia, after having been to Trieste to dispose of the produce of their lands.

As the clocks struck five, we steamed out of Trieste on one of the finest mornings that could be imagined. The sea was as smooth as a mirror, and of the most intense blue. How often we stopped as we went down the coast of Istria I cannot tell, as we were constantly heaving to for the convenience of passengers going on shore in boats which put off to receive them; we did stop however at Capo d'Istria, and then at Pirano, where I was able to take a rough sketch of that most picturesque little town, with its beautiful mediæval castle perched on the cliff behind it.

Then we came to Parenzo, where I should very much have liked to go ashore for a couple of hours to look at the cathedral, of which I had heard so much, but unfortunately the little business the steamer had to transact was done in a few minutes, and the Captain would not delay (probably because my bribe was insufficient), so I had to comfort myself with the hope of seeing it on some future occasion, when I trust to be able again to visit all those spots which interested me so much then, as also many other places in the same countries, which accidental circumstances prevented me from seeing.

The Cathedral of Parenzo, which I was so anxious to see, and which had been described to me by a friend at Trieste as a *meraviglia*, was founded by Bishop Eupatius, and completed in the year 526; it is therefore as old as St. Sophia of Constantinople, and older than any other Cathedral in Europe. " It is said to have a semicircular apse behind the altar, with the Bishop's throne, and seats on either side for the clergy, instances of which are now so rarely to be met with."* . . . .

"At the east end is a round apse, as glorious in its mosaics as St. Mark's, or St. Sophia. Every part of the wall and rounded roof is covered with mosaics, &c. A group of nine saints and angels surrounding the Blessed Virgin and Child, on a golden background, is exquisitely done. Heads of

* Sir J. G. Wilkinson's " Dalmatia and Montenegro."

saints adorn the arches, all are beautiful. Below these, to about ten feet high, the walls are inlaid with whole shells of mother-of-pearl let into a dark brown stone; it looks just like a piece of Damascus furniture, and though rude it is effective and beautiful.

" The flooring of the whole church is of course mosaic, in Byzantine patterns, the same as in Murano and St. Mark's; but one can scarcely look at anything after the wall mosaics, save the capitals of the columns. The pillars themselves are of a fine brown marble; the capitals are identically the same as those in Santa Sophia, one more exquisitely under-cut than the other into lace-work of leaves, flowers, birds, &c.; they are perhaps a little bolder than those of St. Sophia, but full of life and spirit, not a line wasted nor a thought thrown away. I longed to sketch them, but I could only hope they may one day be photographed; Jerusalem and Constantinople alone can rival them.

" The Baldacchino is exceedingly curious and fine, as are also the very ancient altar hangings. There is a splendid altar front, of solid silver gilt, of the Renaissance date. The interest appertaining to this is that it is placed at the *back* of the altar for high mass, facing the Bishop, who is seated *behind the altar*, as at Torcello ; this is an ancient and I believe unique privilege.

"The Chapel of St. Andrew, at the north-east corner of the church, is very interesting and curious. There has been a porch or cloister at the west entrance, but only two or three columns remain of it. I venture to think this church is well worth a special journey from England to see. I could think of nothing else the rest of the day, although our onward voyage was full of beauty."*

We then came to Rovigno with its beautiful campanile, and here again I could not get half an hour to go on shore to look at it, though I believe there is not much more to be seen beside it.

At three p.m. we came in sight of the harbour of Pola—the Portsmouth of Austria ;—but Pola itself we could not see, as it lies at the bottom of a bay communicating with the sea by a deep

* Lady Strangford's " Eastern Shores of the Adriatic."

and winding channel, apparently well defended by
numerous forts which surround it. The harbour
itself is of very considerable dimensions, and so
deep that the largest vessels can come alongside
the quays.

Although so important a place, there did not
appear to be much life or bustle about it. The
country around it is flat and marshy, and sometimes in the year very unhealthy. It must have
been, however, an important place in the days of
ancient Rome, judging from the size of its amphitheatre, and the beauty of the Temple and
triumphal arches which still remain, and which
constitute after all the great attractions of Pola.
They are quite close to the landing, so they can be
visited with the utmost facility during the stay
which the steamer generally makes there. The
amphitheatre alone is worth a special visit, as the
exterior of it is perfect, and at a short distance does
not even look like a ruin. It dates from the third
century and is very fine. It consists of a base-
ment story about four hundred and thirty feet in
length, by three hundred and fifty feet in width,
surmounted by two tiers of arches, with half columns

of the Tuscan order between each, all about eighty feet high.

Beautifully preserved as is the exterior, the condition of the interior is most disappointing, as nothing remains of the internal arrangement except on one side, the one furthest from the sea, where there are still a few seats cut in the rock, some even bearing what most probably were the initials of their owners carved into them.

What can have caused this utter ruin of all the accommodation for the spectators? Have the natives from time to time removed the building materials from the inside, for the purpose of building the modern town? not daring to lay a sacrilegious hand on the shell of the building itself, which bore no semblance to a ruin, while at the same time they treated the interior as a quarry! or were the seats made of wood-work, and destroyed by fire, as some have imagined?

The steamer always remains long enough to permit the traveller to visit the amphitheatre and the temples, as well as the triumphal arches, and to take a stroll through the Piazza. I did so, and still further improved the passing hour by eating an excellent dinner *al fresco* under a *pergola* of vines at the *Trattoria* of the place.

It was just dark as I got on board again, having been warned by the unmusical steam-whistle that the vessel would soon be under way again. Just before starting, a military band came to play before the Commandant's house, which is on the quays just opposite to where the steamer was moored. It being now dark, the band was accompanied by a score of soldiers carrying a peculiarly shaped lantern fastened to the top of a pole, to enable the men to see their music. At first as the band came marching down the quays with their lights dancing high up in the air before and behind, I could not make out what it was, and only for the liveliness of the music I might have thought it was a funeral, the whole thing was very picturesque and the music excellent. At last we got under way and steamed out of the harbour on our way to the coast of Dalmatia, across the Gulf of the Quarnero, so well known for its dangerous navigation and so much dreaded even by the hardy sailors of the Adriatic, when swept by the fierce impetuous Bora.

Fortunately for me, who am not the most intrepid of mariners, and who prefer admiring a tempestuous sea from off a rocky vantage point upon the shore, to tossing on its stormy waves, the dreaded Quarnero was as smooth as a mill-pond. The night was magnificent; the heavens cloudless, and studded with countless stars, but scarcely as bright as I have seen them at other times, owing to the intense brilliancy of the moon now nearly at the full. The track of the steamer was clearly marked out far in the rear by a broad phosphorescent wake, while the water which was dashed off from the paddles seemed like liquid fire.

The cabins were all occupied, so I had to make my bed on deck; but even if I could have got one, I never could have slept below, it was so hot and stuffy. I was soon settled for the night; a doubled-up rug laid lengthwise on the deck was my bed, and my dressing-bag was my pillow. It was so warm that I required no covering save my light tweed suit, and I was no sooner down than I was fast asleep. I don't know how long I slept; but I would have slept still longer, if I had not been awoke by the steamer stopping to put down and take up passengers and goods at some place on the coast of Dalmatia.

We had safely crossed the mouth of the Quarnero, the moon had set, and the blue black vault of heaven was studded with countless stars sparkling like diamonds. The steamer was hove to a little distance from the shore, while scores of boats, each with a coloured lantern at the prow, came and went, making as pretty a scene as can be imagined ; but for all that, after sitting up and admiring it for a few minutes, I lay down again on my rug, and falling asleep never awoke again till the sun was high in the heavens the next morning.

By degrees the passengers one by one came on deck, when by making interest with Giovanni, the steward, I obtained the use of a *camerino* (cabin) to make my toilet in. Having completed my ablutions I called in Giovanni to empty my tub, for as the *camerino* was extremely small it was next to impossible to stand in it, unless with one's feet in the water. Never was steward so astonished and so puzzled as Giovanni was at the sight of my flimsy mackintosh tub; he had no idea of how to take it up to empty it, he was afraid to touch it until I had taken it up on three sides and showed him how to lift it, when he was so delighted with the whole arrangement that he placed it on the table of the cabin just as it was, and fetched down the passengers to see the ingenious English device. By the time it had been well examined and then emptied, I was up and dressed. When I came out of the *camerino*, I showed the assembled company how it could be rolled up into the smallest compass, and stowed away in a travelling bag.

There was no regular breakfast on board, but everyone as he wanted it got a cup of coffee and a bit of bread or a biscuit; preserved milk also could be had, but of butter there was none.

Our passengers had somewhat varied since leaving Trieste. We had deposited many on the coast of Istria as we went along, and taken up others in their place. We had a remarkable Oriental-look-ing woman, plain perhaps, and yet handsome, a

Montenegrin of rank, a cousin of the present Prince, dressed in full native costume. She was on her way to her native country to petition the Prince to permit certain of his cousins, who had been expatriated for political causes, to return to their homes.

The costume of the Montenegrin women is not becoming ; even this handsome woman, and the beautiful Princess whom I subsequently had the honour of seeing at Montenegro, failed to render it attractive to my eyes, whereas the costume of the men is eminently becoming. This lady's dress consisted of a sort of white chemise of fine lawn, tight, but gathered very full round the neck, without any frill, and open down the front for six or eight inches, where it was closed by a row of very small buttons. This white garment, which reached down to the ankles, was fastened round her waist by a massive silver belt, made in compartments three inches by four and joined together by hinges. Each compartment was highly ornamented with rich *repoussé* work in *alto rilievo*, and from a side-piece hung down several ornaments of the châtelaine species, while from the other side depended an exquisite little dagger in a sheath of silver *repoussé*.

The sleeves of this white garment were tight at the shoulders, but grew wider and wider as they approached the wrist, where they were upwards of two feet six inches in diameter. They were bordered with a rich margin of embroidery in gold and silver thread, mingled with red and blue silk, in excellent taste, and the same embroidery was continued up the external seam of the sleeve on the outside of the elbow up to the shoulder. From below the silver belt she wore a large apron of rich black silk coming down to her ankles, and over all a peculiar white cloth coat without sleeves, the typical garment of the Montenegrins, both male and female. This coat was made of a very soft white cloth, so close and yet soft and pliable, that although sitting next to her and touching it with my finger, I could not at once determine if it was cloth or some sort of beautifully tanned leather. As I said before, this coat was without sleeves or collar, but scooped tight to the back of the neck. In front it did not come further forward than about half way

between the point of the shoulders and the middle
of the neck, and then straight down like a sack
till just below the calf of the leg. This coat was
bound right round the whole way with a narrow
pattern of embroidery in the same style as round
the sleeves of the muslin dress, and in addition
had a row of very small round silver buttons down
the front on one side. On her head she wore a
very large black Indian silk kerchief fastened into
her hair with pins, and hanging down behind her
back as low as her waist.

The costume is decidedly ugly, though containing the elements of great beauty, if only put
together with taste and harmony. Nothing, for
instance, can be more attractive and becoming than
that black kerchief, be it of silk, gauze or lace,
when gracefully put on the head, as the women
of Spain or Genoa know so well how to wear it;
but the Montenegrin arrangement is as clumsy
and inelegant in the women as it is manly and
picturesque in the men.

We had on board also several Austrian officers
going to join their quarters, some to Zara and
some to Cattaro, Budua, and Kosmatch. Very

nice, pleasant, gentlemanlike fellows they were, some of them speaking French, but all able to converse freely in Italian, and all well-informed, agreeable companions. Acquaintances are made much more easily abroad than in England, so we were soon quite at home together, and what with chatting, smoking and walking up and down the deck, we quickly passed over the time, till at ten o'clock a.m., we came in front of Zara, celebrated in ancient times for its long siege, when "in 1346 Marino Faliero earned his laurels by the most daring assault," and in modern times for its excellent Maraschino!

Zara is an important place even at the present time. It is the capital of Dalmatia, and the seat of the Archibishop of the province. It is well-built, clean, and tolerably well-paved, and well-worth a visit. The time, however, allowed by the stay of the steamer is amply sufficient to enable one to see it; but the heat was so great that I felt more inclined to stay on board smoking cigarettes under the awning of the steamer than to go on shore. The prospect of some *café à la glace*, however, which I knew was to be obtained in the Piazza, added to the more important fact that I was to receive here a letter for the Archimandrite of Montenegro, induced me to shake off my apathy.

Having landed on the quay, I passed through the gate over which is sculptured the grim effigy of the Lion of St. Mark, everywhere seen down the Eastern shores of the Adriatic wheresoever the Venetians had established their authority, I proceeded to execute my plans; but the heat was so intense that I was glad to come back to the steamer where I imagined it was something less stifling. But this day was unusually hot and close, and with the exception of one at Cattaro, when the the thermometer registered at four o'clock p.m., 105° Fahrenheit, was the hottest I experienced in all my journey.

CHAPTER VI.

T about one o'clock P.M. we steamed
away from Zara while we were at
dinner, and at five P.M. reached Sebenico.   Should I ever travel again in
that part of the world, I think I should try to go
from Zara to Sebenico by land in order to see the
ruins of Asseria, which I learnt afterwards were
well worth a visit; but the journey should in that
case be undertaken earlier in the year, to avoid the
oppressive heats.

The afternoon between leaving Zara and arriving at Sebenico passed quickly away, for I had the advantage of two most agreeable companions; one the capuchin monk, the other a charming young fellow, an officer in an Austrian Jäger regiment, Baron Heyd von Heydeg.

The Capuchin was a most interesting man, and we chatted many an hour together by moonlight on the deck, when every one else had gone to sleep, when I used to chaff him about the rules of his order, which forbid the smoking of tobacco, while they permit the use of snuff without any restriction. He used to take it most good-humouredly, and laughed as if his sides would split when I would refuse to take a pinch of his snuff unless he smoked one of my cigarettes. I verily think I should have brought him round at last, had he not been constantly under the surveillance, and in mortal "*soggezione*" of his lay brother.

Heyd was a different fellow altogether, but most agreeable. He was going to join his regiment, then quartered at Budua. We travelled together as far as Cattaro, and I met him subsequently both at Cettigne and Budua, where I went expressly to pay him a visit.

The time sped swiftly and most agreeably in spite of the heat, and at five o'clock P.M. we steamed through the narrow tortuous opening, bordered by steep rocky sides, which leads into the bay, at the furthur end of which stands Sebenico. It is a noble harbour, and so deep that a frigate can lie alongside the quay. At the narrowest part of its entrance, the approach is defended by what a few years ago would have been considered a masterpiece of fortification, but which at present would offer too fair a target to our projectiles to afford any great protection against an enemy. It is still worth a visit, as its case-mates are perhaps among the finest in the world. It was engineered and built in 1546, by the cele-brated architect San Micheli. The entrance to the fortress is surmounted by the usual Venetian Lion with the following inscription :—

" Pax tibi Marce Evangelista meus."*

---

* In August, 1647, a Pasha of Bosnia, pouring an army of 30,000 men into the lowlands, attempted the capture of Sebenico and its

Having landed with Baron Heyd, who had been quartered there some time before, for cicerone, I pro-proceeded to inspect the Duomo, or cathedral, the principal object of interest there. Some people are lost in admiration of this cathedral, I really could not see much about it to admire, and the two statues on its façade representing Adam and Eve (they might as well be Gog and Magog) are simply detestable. But the roof of the cathedral is a curiosity in itself, and worth the journey. It is of its kind unique, and though it is said to be perfectly safe, and I suppose must be so, having continued so for so many years, still I could not help feeling a sense of insecurity as long as I was in the church, and enjoyed great relief when I finally came out of it.

This roof is simply a semi-cylinder made of enormous slabs of stone joined edge to edge, but so beautifully adapted and fitted one into the other that, without any other support save what they afford each other, they form the vault of this

fort; but it was so well defended by the 6000 Venetians and German mercenaries of the garrison, that after twenty-six days' cannonade the Pasha was obliged to retire.

cathedral. I trust they may never crack; but I, for one, could never say my prayers with comfort under such a roof.

Having taken a ramble through the streets, which were clean and contained many fine mansions, we went up to the fort on the hill behind the town, and which commands the whole place, where we passed a pleasant hour with the officers of the garrison.

My time being limited, I was unable to make an expedition from Sebenico, which under different circumstances I should certainly have undertaken, that is to the falls of the Kerka and the monastery above them. My friend, the Capuchin, who had travelled a good deal both in Europe and America, and had a good eye for the picturesque, told me they were well worth seeing; but like many other interesting spots down that coast, I must only hope to visit them at some future time.

At dusk we returned to the steamer, though we knew it would not leave till the following morning early, and we could have spent a most pleasant night on shore; but Sebenico shuts its gates at sunset, and then till the following sunrise no one can come in or go out, and had we attempted it we should only have lost our passage.

Having partaken of an excellent supper, I returned to the deck, where, as was my wont, I sat down beside my friend the Capuchin, who always took a cup of coffee with me though he would not consent to smoke. We chatted till very late, when he went down to his *camerino*, and I settled myself on deck as usual for my night's sleep. It turned out awfully hot, as the steamer remained till break of day in the harbour of Sebenico, but what must it have been in the cabin?

At the very earliest dawn we left our moorings, and steamed out of the harbour by its well guarded entrance. Just outside we passed a group of small islands, among which is established a considerable coral fishery. The coral is not however of the finest quality, mostly of the common deep red kind, and is principally sold on the spot or at the fair of Sinigaglia in the Romagna on the opposite or Italian side of the Adriatic.

The dawn was just merging into daylight, when

we steamed out of that land-locked harbour. It had been stiflingly hot as long as we had lain still alongside the quay, but the moment we came out into the open sea, the

> " . . . . Aura messaggiera . . . .
> Ad annunziar che se ne vien l'Aurora,"

came with a most refreshing breeze, so light, however, as not even to raise a "cat's paw" on the glassy waters, but still deliciously cool and invigorating.

The steward was not long manufacturing me a good cup of coffee, after which, having made myself comfortable in a capital arm-chair, I again went to sleep, not to awake until Giovanni summoned me again, "per far colazione."

In the course of the morning we reached Spalato, a beautiful and most interesting place, where an artist could with advantage spend many days. It was celebrated in ancient times for the gorgeous palace which the Emperor Diocletian built for himself after abdicating the Empire in 303 A.D., and the magnificent remains of which still form the glory of the present city. After a reign of twenty years, "Diocletian executed his memorable resolution of abdicating the Empire," and acquired the glory of giving to the world the most remarkable, if not the first, example of a resignation which has not been very frequently imitated by succeeding monarchs. Withdrawing to Salona, he passed the last nine years of his life in seclusion—the building of a palace in the neighbourhood, and the superintendence of his garden, occupying his leisure hours. The satisfaction he derived from these pursuits is sufficiently proved by his well-known answer to Maximian, when urging him to re-assume the purple, "If I could show you the cabbages I have planted with my own hands at Salona, you would no longer urge me to relinquish the enjoyment of happiness for the pursuit of power."

This immense palace, which covered very nearly nine English acres of ground, was almost a perfect square terminating at the four corners by a quadrangular tower. Its faces were directed as nearly as possible to the four cardinal points—the southern side being pointed to the shore and facing the sea. It still exists in good preservation and forms a grand object of attraction to the visitor entering the harbour. Two streets intersected each other at right angles nearly in the centre of it, which has lately been completely excavated and is now fully exposed to view.

The following description by the late Mr. Paton (author of " Highlands and Islands of the Adriatic," one of the most charming books ever printed) will convey to the reader a far clearer impression than anything I could pen; I therefore make no apology for inserting it here, and whoever should wish to go still deeper into the matter and learn all that is to be learned concerning this palace, I refer him to Mr. Adams' book " Spalato Restored," which is a perfectly exhaustive treatise on the subject.

" At the outset we are struck with the enormous extent of the palace, which is not less than nine acres and a half; so that even Constantine Porphyrogenitus speaks of it with admiration, as one of the greatest edifices then extant. In the time of Diocletian, his great retinue and a pretorian cohort could be lodged with convenience in it. Sixteen towers gave strength and elegance to the edifice, of which the largest were those at the four corners. The back of the edifice looked to the north-east on the land-side, and there was the principal entrance, the Porta Aurea, or golden gate, which led to the Peristylium, a great court of granite columns; and the cross street which intersected the principal passage at right angles was terminated at each end by gates, the one the Porta Ferrea, or iron gate, the other the Porta Ænea, or gate of brass, which are so called to this day.

" This peristylium, or court of granite columns, was flanked by two temples; the greater of Jupiter, and the smaller of Esculapius; the former, a lofty octagon, was ascended by a stair of fifteen steps; an uneven number being generally found in the temples of the ancients, that, beginning to move with the right foot, they might, of course, place it first upon the uppermost step in order to enter the temple—a form which was accounted respectful in approaching the Deity. From the peristylium, or court of granite columns, the Roman entered the principal inhabited part of the palace; first was the porticus of Corinthian order, then the circular dome-covered vestibulum, with the Lares and Penates; then the atrium, or quadrangular hall, ninety-eight by forty-five with its arms and trophies dedicated to ancestry; and last of all the crypto-porticus, or grand gallery, looking to the south-west, thus facing the sea, and forming a noble promenade of five hundred and fifteen feet in length, in which, during the heat of Summer or inclemency of Winter, the Emperor could take exercise. This crypto-porticus was the principal feature of the palace, and the well-known taste of Diocletian leads us to suppose that the choicest statuary and paintings of the Old World must have adorned its walls. The relics of Pompeii give some idea of the classic fancy in ornament, the harmonizing contrasts in colour, and the consummate skill in tessellation employed in the domestic architecture of the ancients; and if we relieve these splendours with the latest fascination in the unpretending forms of Greek statuary, how puny is the utmost magnificence of Versailles compared with the dwelling of the retired Roman!

"Such was the Palace of Diocletian; what now remains of the edifice? The shell or outer wall, of which the best preserved part is the grand gallery facing the sea; for Spalato like its contemporary Baalbec being used as a fortification, the rough stone and mortar of the middle-age battlements surmount in many places the massive normal masonry of the Roman Empire. . . . Within the town, fragments of Roman architecture are scattered thickly enough, but so obscured and mingled with modern houses as to present a mass of confusion."

Did we stop short here, the reader might well imagine that beyond the shell, the walls which surrounded the palace, nothing has been preserved; such however is not the case, and I shall now endeavour to describe what I saw in Spalato the morning that I steamed into its harbour, when from the deck of my vessel I gazed on that sea studded all over with numberless boats spreading the most fantastic sails to the gentlest of breezes!

The prevailing form, if not the only one, was the lateen in all its varieties, most of the boats carrying but one. But such colours and such devices painted on them! things that would look simply outrageous at Cowes or Ryde, how lovely they seemed there! Some were striped from above downwards with every colour of the rainbow, but only two colours to each sail and these always harmoniously contrasted; others of one uniform colour, with some fantastic ornament in sharp contrast in the middle; while some, all of one colour had at the topmost angle of the lateen a representation of the sun generally in burnished gold with its rays coming down a long way over the sail. The glittering golden sea, those fairy-looking boats gliding over it, the picturesque costumes of the sailors, the whole scene bathed in that golden light was a fit preparation for my introduction to the rare beauties of Spalato itself.

As we slowly approached the quay, there was ample time to admire the long façade of Diocletian's Palace, with the tall and elegant campanile which rises inside it on the right, and the strong hexagonal machicolated tower on the left. The lofty steeple on the right, a very Giralda of elegance and airiness—the dungeon on the left a sturdy emblem of the iron-fisted middle ages.

After some customary formalities, during which I feasted my eyes on the picturesque groups that crowded on the quay, permission was finally given to go ashore; when crossing as quickly as could be the narrow intervening space, I plunged through the Porta Ferrea into the vaulted passage which on this side gives entrance to the city of Spalato; and now commence the real difficulties of description, but having undertaken it I must only try, trusting to the kind forbearance of my readers.

This vaulted entrance is narrow, perhaps not twelve feet wide, but very lofty and formed of immense blocks of stone put together with wonderful accuracy. After following it a little way, it opens out into a spacious round hall rising up to a considerable height, this portion being unroofed; from it open out several streets, all running about here and there, crossing and recrossing each other as if in search of light and air. The dwellings in these streets are full of quaint artistic beauty; at one point one meets a massive wall of square-cut blocks dating from the days of Diocletian, against which, perhaps, is built up a modern house with wrought-iron balconies of the most delicate workmanship; further on, an outside staircase of rude stone steps, partly covered with a roof of russet tiles, leads to a door some thirty feet above our heads, from which a flying buttress crosses over to an opening in an ancient wall beyond, where a modern habitation has been constructed in some mediæval donjon.

Each turn brings a new surprise, and so one passes on till one comes to the piazza, and this day being a festival, it swarmed with natives from all the surrounding *campagne.* The reader must now come with me to the *café*, where under a thick awning and surrounded by a screen of oleanders and orange-trees in full bloom, we shall take a *granita di caffé* (a water-ice flavoured with coffee), and study the moving panorama before us, whilst we slowly puff away a cigarette made with the ambrosial tobacco of Trebigna—a kind still unknown in London and in Paris!

CHAPTER VII.

SITTING down cross-legged on the very oldest and dirtiest of rugs, and just outside our fragrant hedge of oleander, is to be seen an old Jew, the finest type of a Shylock that could be imagined; with ample, heavy, flowing beard, aquiline nose with sharp cut nostril, and deep-set piercing eyes shadowed by an ample turban. He has before him, on his rug, a collection of arms, pistols of the old approved Turkish form and yataghans of every price, from the common horn-handled weapon in a wooden sheath to the jewel-hilted Kharjar in a sheath of *repoussé* silver. Around is a motley group of countrymen, all talking at the top of their voices in their several languages, whilst examining and praising or depreciating the weapons there for sale, just as they are either simple *flâneurs* in the square, or really intending purchasers. The varieties of costume rendered this picturesque group most interesting, there were Morlacchi from the neighbouring mountains with full blue Turkish trowsers fast to the knee; gold embroidered crimson jackets without sleeves, and gaiters to match ; the whole finished off by an immense Albanian scarf of many colours wound round the waist, holding a perfect armoury of weapons in the front. On the head most of them wore a small red fez, others wore a turban, but it was not put on like the Jews, they did not seem *au fait* in settling it ; but whatever head-gear they adopted they all were decorated with a tail—a genuine plaited tail coming down their backs with such luxuriance that it might have been the envy of any Celestial. I could not bring myself to like it—though report says that the Morlacchi are wonderfully attached to their tails, and cherish and pet them somewhat in the manner of our old tars in the days of Collingwood and Nelson.

There were Turks from the Herzegovina, ill-looking, badly-clad, scowling Mussulmans, who would willingly have earned ten paras by sending a Christian to his latter home, but still gorgeous in their tatters and vermin. There were Christian Albanians with their white fustanellas, high aquiline nose, glittering eyes, and false smile, in dress somewhat similar to the Morlacchi, but wearing a smaller fez with a long blue tassel. Conspicuous above them all was a Risanese from the Gulf of Cattaro, in full Montenegrin costume; but with a green instead of the white characteristic coat, all overladen about the breast and shoulders with plates of solid gold of considerable thickness, especially over the shoulders, where they would, if required, afford some protection from the blow of a sabre.

Mingled with the men were several women— some very good-looking—with golden-brown hair and dark eyes and eyelashes; their hair in plaits, not hanging but coiled round their heads, which were further adorned with Turkish piastres and other coins. The dress is a mixture of red, white, and blue artistically combined, with coral and coins twisted round their necks.

The noise of this Babel of tongues was deafening, and the scene not to be described. One wretched, tattered old man, but armed to the teeth like the rest, long tried to persuade me to buy a hank of onions, and would not be gainsaid when told by one of the waiters of the *café* that I was a traveller and did not require onions; what better or more portable provisions could I carry with me in my travels than onions? said he.

Having finished my *granita*, I again started to explore the city; this time under the guidance of a most obliging gentleman, well versed in the antiquities of the place, and to whom I had brought an introduction. We first went outside the city to inspect the grand Porta Aurea. This had only lately been thoroughly excavated, and even in its present dilapidated condition, not so much the effect of time as of the plundering propensities of man, is still most beautiful and grand. What must it have been before the eight columns which decorated its front were taken away to adorn some modern church?

From the Porta Aurea, we again got into the city, proceeding straight to the court of the vestibule of the Palace, where all that is best worth seeing in Spalato is collected together. Here in front of us was the façade of the peristyle, consisting of four large and beautiful granite columns, supporting a triangular pediment, and which occupied the whole breadth of the court. On each side were a row of six Corinthian columns, equally large, and also of rose-coloured Egyptian granite, supporting not an architrave as is generally the case, but a series of arches which sprang from their capitals. On the right was the smaller temple, dedicated to Esculapius, now converted into a baptistry, and dedicated to St. John. On the left, the Temple of Jupiter—now the Cathedral of Spalato, by the side of which rises that most elegant campanile, the Giralda of Spalato, only one hundred and ninety-nine feet high, since the two upper stories were thrown down by lightning.

The interior of the Cathedral does not offer much to admire—nevertheless its general effect is sufficiently imposing. But it is outside in the court, the present piazza, that all the beauty of the place reveals itself. It is not a ruin—of the sixteen original granite columns not one has been displaced, and this portion of the Palace of Spalato is as in the days when Diocletian came into his Temple to pray. Can the reader believe that all this is really within five days of London?

Dalmatia has been the birthplace of many men of letters and science, and Spalato can boast of having even given a Protestant Dean to our royal Windsor, in the person of the celebrated Mark Anthony de Dominis, once Catholic Archbishop of Spalato, whose life and death would furnish materials for a sensational novel. As his history is not commonly known, it may, perhaps, interest some of my readers to hear it now.

He was born about the year 1570, and educated at the Illyrian College of the Jesuits, in Loretto, from whence he passed to Padua, where he became Professor of Mathematics. In the year 1600, he

was created Bishop of Segna, and in 1602 he was
raised to the Archbishopric of Spalato, where,
during the terrible plague of 1607, he nobly distinguished himself by his liberality to the poor, and
his fearless and humane attendance on the sick in
the administration of his sacerdotal duties—emu-
lating the courage and devotion, under similar
circumstances, of Borromeo of Milan. He occupied
the Archiepiscopal throne of Spalato for fourteen
years, during which period his time was divided
between the performance of his ecclesiastical duties,
and the investigations of science. He converted
the upper part of the Palace, at Spalato, into a
Laboratory and an Observatory, and the window
is still shown where he is supposed to have made
the discovery of the prismatic colour of light, " by
the falling drops of water;" which discovery, including a description of the nature of the rainbow,
he published to the world in a work printed at
Venice in 1611. His fickleness in matters of
religion, however, proved his ruin; his Chapter
accused him of heretical opinions, upon which he
withdrew to Venice at the close of 1615, having
previously vacated his See in favour of his nephew

Sforza Ponsoni. During his residence in that city, he wrote a work in favour of the Republic, which was condemned by the Inquisition, when he determined on withdrawing, for safety, to a Protestant country.

He went first to Heidelberg, and thence came to England in the suite and at the invitation of Sir Henry Wotton, Ambassador of James I. to the Venetian Republic. In England, he published and dedicated to James I. a history of the Council of Trent, which had been lent him, it is said, by its author, Fra Paolo Sarpi. He also edified the Protestant public by an open recantation of his religion in St. Paul's Cathedral, and then published a work against the Papacy, entitled, " Scoglio del Naufragio Christiano." He was particularly well received in England ; and was patronized by the King, who made him Dean of Windsor. He seems, however, to have expected more, and to have been disappointed at not getting a bishopric ; and on Gregory XV, who was a friend and relative of his, succeeding him to the Papal throne, he changed his religion again, and yielding to the solicitations of the Pope, conveyed to him through the Spanish Ambassador, who promised him a Cardinal's Hat, he returned to Rome in 1622.

Gregory XV. received him kindly, and as long as he lived De Dominis remained unmolested, but at his death Pope Urban VIII., who succeeded him, saw no reason to extend his protection over the ex-Protestant Dean of Windsor; he was accused of heresy, handed over to the tender mercies of the Holy Inquisition, and thrown into a dungeon of the Castle of St. Angelo, where he died in 1625 —it is supposed by poison, and his body was subsequently burned, together with his writings, in the Campo dei Fiori.

De Dominis was a very distinguished philosopher, and we must not be too severe when judging him by the light of the present day. There can be no doubt that the change from Popery to the Reformed religion was principally due, not to a feeling of animosity against the Church of Rome, as many have maintained, but chiefly to those doubts concerning the truth of the things taught by that church, and to its conduct in persisting to refuse the results of the investigations of science, as evinced by its treatment of Galileo and others.

His return to the church is more difficult to account for on generous grounds; but he, himself, is stated to have said that by becoming a Cardinal he might be of greater use in effecting a reformation in that community to which he had originally belonged. The Holy Inquisition had hoped to have enjoyed the satisfaction of publicly roasting, " ad majorem Dei gloriam," a professor of Natural Science, a renegade Catholic Archbishop and a Protestant Dean all in one; but some charitable friend robbed that holy confraternity of its anticipated triumph by passing in some poison to the unfortunate De Dominis, who learnt too late that Rome never changes, "che il Lupo perde il pelo, il vizio no" and that according to Papal ethics to keep faith with heretics is at best a grievous sin.

Spalato, in common with the rest of Dalmatia, has given birth to many able men, among which they claim even St. Jerome, the most learned of the ancient fathers and the talented author of the noblest translation of the Bible; but I fear on insufficient grounds, as all the authorities I have looked into seem to make him a Pannonian and not an Illyrian; Carrara, however, claims him as a compatriot in his " Uomini Illustri di Spalato."

Within a few miles of Spalato are the ruins of
Salona, I had not time to visit them.   There is not
comparatively very much of interest to be seen
above ground, but I believe that methodically
conducted diggings have yielded some valuable
results.   It was the Roman capital of Dalmatia and
was destroyed by the Avars in 640, when the
inhabitants who escaped from the slaughter took
refuge in Spalato and there founded the new city,
by grouping themselves around and under the
protection of the Palace of Diocletian.

The majority of the inhabitants of Spalato are
Roman Catholics, with an admixture of Greeks and
a good number of Jews, who wear the turban and
the Oriental costume, and are principally descended
from those who were expelled from Spain in 1493.
For many centuries they were subjected to the same
indignities as in other Christian countries, and compelled to inhabit the Ghetto where they used to be
locked up at night; but such practices have long
been abolished in Dalmatia, and the Jews of Spalato
have enjoyed for many years the same privileges as
the other citizens of that place.

My stay at Spalato was much too short for enjoyment; I saw indeed most that was to be seen there, but it was not much more than a glance, and I longed to be sketching amongst those picturesque nooks.

Having several times mentioned the Morlacchi, it will, I think, be interesting to my readers to know something about them. Again I have to regret that I was unable to visit them in their villages, and that the only information I can give of them is, that they are inhabitants of the wild mountainous district lying to the East of Dalmatia. They are a fine race of men, though much smaller and inferior to the Montenegrin; their women, on the contrary, are often very beautiful, and they have many strange customs in their dealings with foreigners which would make an excursion into the fastnesses of their mountains of more than ordinary interest.

With the Lowland Dalmatians and the inhabitants of the towns on the coast, the name of Morlacchi is always associated with plunder and cattle-lifting, just as in Scotland a hundred years ago every Highlander, in the eyes of a Lowlander, was a cateran and a robber; but I heard from people that had been among them, that they are very hospitable, and that their country can be freely traversed in any direction without the smallest danger.   They are Catholics and apparently of the same stock as the Montenegrins, though these latter are schismatic Greeks.

CHAPTER VIII.

EARLY in the afternoon we left Spalato, and steaming away from the coast we stood out to sea, making for Lissa, a large island of the Adriatic, celebrated in the days of the first Napoleon for the stout sea fight in which, on the 13th of March 1811, Captain Hoste, (afterwards Sir William Hoste), with four ships mounting 156 guns, utterly defeated the French fleet of twenty-seven sail, mounting 284, having on board 500 troops. In 1808 we occupied Lissa, and having established free trade and other institutions, the island improved so much under our administration that in less than three years from the time we occupied it the population had risen to 12,000 inhabitants (at present it has scarcely 5000).

The French were naturally sorely tried by the advantageous position we occupied in front of their coast, and the very good use we made of our opportunities of pushing our commerce in every direction. They determined therefore on expelling us from Lissa and the Adriatic, as from the smallness of our armament there they had no doubt as to their success. Swiftly and silently they fitted out an expedition at Ancona, which under the command of the brave Captain Dubourdieu arrived at Lissa on the 13th March, 1811. It consisted of four 44 gun frigates, ten 32 gun corvettes, one 16 gun brig, a schooner, ten gun-boats, and a xebeque, in all 284 guns.

The British Squadron consisted of only four ships, the 'Amphion,' 'Active,' 'Cerberus,' and 'Volage,' mounting but 156 guns all told, but it was commanded and manned by British seamen! the result could not be doubted, and although Dubourdieu fought like a gallant sailor as he was, the victory remained with us. Our losses were severe, and in a quiet retired little nook, on the left hand as one enters the land-locked harbour of Lissa, are buried those who fell in that engagement; while on the right hand side is another burial place, where under a handsome sepulchral monument lie the remains of those Austrians who fell in the latest naval engagement at Lissa when a few years ago the Italian Navy, the pet toy, an expensive one by the by, of King Victor Emmanuel, was all but annihilated by the Austrians under Admiral Tegethoff.

At Lissa we remained a very short time, so short that I had not even time to go ashore, though I should have very much liked to visit the burial place of those brave English sailors who fell in the naval action of 1811. The business of the steamer, which seemed principally to consist in shipping a bridal party, was soon concluded, and after a very short stay we were again under full steam for Lesina, another island of the same archipelago, but much smaller and closer in to the Dalmatian coast.

The bridal party we had taken on board consisted of the bride and bridegroom, both very plain and very much, even tawdrily over-dressed in Parisian costume, and with remarkably dirty hands and otherwise unwashed appearance. A bishop with a couple of priests in attendance on his reverence, and half-a-dozen relations and friends of the newly-married couple, who seemed principally to study not to take any notice of each other but went about making themselves generally agreeable.

The groom most kindly insisted on my smoking his cigars (and villainously bad they were, but had I declined them he would have been awfully offended) and drinking his maraschino, which fortunately was as good as his cigars were bad, whilst the bride, luckily for me, persistently avoided me, probably from fear of heretical contamination, and exclusively devoted her attentions to the Bishop and his priests.

After a few hours steaming through the smoothest and bluest of seas, in full view of the grand mountains of Dalmatia, in due time we arrived at Lesina a little before sunset. This island is said to derive its name from being somewhat shaped like an awl, in Italian *lesina*. It is just a thin strip of land forty-two miles long, blunt at one end (which represents the handle) and sharp at the other. I doubt, however, the correctness of its etymology, and am inclined to think that its present name is more probably derived from its ancient one of " Pharos Insula," often reduced by elision into simply " Insula ;" now the anagram of " Insula " is " Lusina," a word much more in harmony with the genius of the Italian language, and from Lusina to Lesina is but a shade. I think I am fortified in this etymology by the fact of at least two other instances in the Adriatic of this identical transposition of letters, and the conversion of Insula to Lusina, in the names of two islands near the Quarnero, named respectively Lussin Grande and Lussin Piccolo, which are evidently the anagram of Insula Grande and Insula Piccola.

We arrived just in time to enjoy the effect of the setting sun upon that rocky landscape and the exquisitely pretty town at the foot of the mountain, and sufficiently early to be able to take a rapid sketch just as the sun was beginning to sink behind the tower which rises to the west of the town. The fort behind and above the town was still in full sunlight, as was also the more distant fortress of San Niccolo, brought forcibly into relief by a bank of dark purple clouds which were massed behind it. Down below, close to the water's edge, lay the town bathed in a flood of amber light, partly caused by the reflection of the golden sunset beyond, and partly by the colouring of the town itself, the houses of which are all painted with the warmest tints.

In the middle of the town, close to the water's edge, are the "Loggie" or Portico, an elegant building, which in the olden times of Venetian supremacy was used by the merchants as an exchange to transact business in, as well as a hall of justice for the administration of the laws, and at the back a room is still shown where criminals and suspected persons underwent the question by torture.

Immediately behind and above the Loggie rises

Fort Spagnuolo, built by Charles V, connected with the town below by two long crenelated walls, enclosing in front a considerable space planted thick with colossal aloes (*Agave Americana*), which in case of assault would, in olden times, have offered a very considerable impediment to the advance of troops.

The island of Lesina is barren, and its commerce very insignificant; it grows, however, an immense quantity of rosemary, from which is distilled a celebrated essential oil *Oleum Anthos*, and the *Aqua Regia*, or rosemary water, which are both largely exported.

It was dark when we left; shaping our way for Curzola where we arrived about midnight. My friend, the Capuchin, who sat chatting with me till we arrived there, regretted I could not see it by daylight, as contrary to the other islands, which are conspicuous for their barrenness, Curzola is well wooded, and is celebrated for the size and magnificence of its pine trees.

We did not make any long delay here, and were soon threading our course again between the islands and the mainland in the direction of Ragusa, but I know nothing about them. The Monk wished me good-night and went to his cabin, when again I took my usual place on deck, and was soon as comfortably asleep on that oaken plank as if I had been in the most luxurious bed in England.

I was awakened from my night's sleep by my friend the Capuchin monk, who had been my travelling companion all the way from Trieste.

"Get up, my lazy friend," said he, touching me with his foot. "We shall soon be entering the port of Gravosa; and there," stretching out his arm towards the Dalmatian coast, "is the island of Lachroma, once the property of the unfortunate Emperor Maximilian of Mexico, and in ancient times a harbour of refuge to your great King Richard, Cœur-de-Lion."

Hard though my bed had been, for nothing but my doubled up old rug had interposed between myself and the deck, I had slept profoundly, "*à la belle étoile*," and far more comfortably than if I had condescended to take my place in the dirty and stuffy *camerino* down below, where all the other passengers, including my friend the Capuchin and his lay-brother, fearing bad smells, fleas, and other small game much less than the delicious night-air of the balmy Adriatic, had carefully stowed themselves away the previous night. I was up in an instant, and I shall not easily forget the sight that greeted my eyes from the deck of the little 'San Carlo.'

We were about three miles from the shore; the sun, though high above the horizon, had not yet acquired sufficient force to destroy the freshness of the morning breeze which delicately rippled the surface of the sea, making it in the sunshine like a sheet of frosted gold, while in the shade it was like liquid sapphire. On my left rose the wild, rocky cliffs of Dalmatia, rendered still more desolate-looking by the almost total absence of vegetation; while in front and on my right, stretching away to the extreme verge of the horizon, were the sparkling waters of the Adriatic, thickly studded with countless islets, to the nearest of which, Lachroma, the Monk had drawn my attention.

"It is now many years," said the Capuchin,

"since your great crusading King found a refuge in that island."

"I was not aware that King Richard was shipwrecked here," said I. "I knew that he met with a terrific storm in this sea on his return from Palestine, but I always imagined he had been wrecked near the top of the Adriatic, on the coast of Istria, in the neighbourhood of Aquileia."

"Yes," replied the Monk, "it is not generally known that it was on the rocks of Lachroma that Cœur-de-Lion was cast away; and it is strange how this error should have crept into history and held its ground and place in every standard work, including your own invaluable Cyclopædias. But we have ample proofs of the truth of what I am telling you, and documentary evidence to establish the accuracy of my assertion; for your King, in gratitude to Divine Providence for delivering him from shipwreck, vowed to build a church in honour of the Blessed Virgin, on whatever land he should first set foot, and having safely landed at Lachroma, he proceeded to make good his vow by committing to the abbot and monks of a

Benedictine monastery, which already existed on the island, the task of building this church, to defray the expenses of which the good King devoted no less than 100,000 *nummi argentei*, which sum he borrowed from his British lieges. But the Rettore of Ragusa (so the President of that ancient Republic was styled), having heard of King Richard's shipwreck opposite his city, went to visit him in state, with all the magistrates and councillors of the Republic, and invited him to Ragusa, where he was received with every demonstration of respect, and all the hospitality and attention due to so distinguished a guest.

King Richard, pleased at the reception given him by the Republicans, and charmed by the attractive graces of the Ragusan ladies, rested there for some time; and then at the suggestion of these fair ones and the urgent entreaties of the authorities, who promised to obtain a dispensation for him from the Pope, he altered the terms of his donation, and founded in Ragusa itself the church to the Blessed Virgin which he had originally vowed on the island of Lachroma; on the condition, however, that the Benedictine Abbot of Lachroma, assisted by the

monks of his convent, should have the privilege
and the right to celebrate mass in this church in
Ragusa every year on the day of the feast of the
Purification. The gift of Richard Cœur-de-Lion
having been further increased by donations from the
inhabitants, this votive church grew into that
celebrated cathedral which for so many years held
the first rank among all the churches of Illyria.*

* The brave King Richard, having recruited himself at Ragusa, is
said, by some, to have gone to Aquileia by sea, by others to have
continued his journey by land; anyhow, it is pretty certain, that
having stopped to take some refreshment at a way-side inn in the
mountains of Dalmatia, or Styria, he incautiously handed a large
gold piece to the landlady to change, and her suspicions being roused
by this circumstance, she informed the authorities; and the end was
that the King was seized by the treacherous Leopold of Austria, and
imprisoned, as everyone knows. There is a tradition, however, which
is not so well known, that shortly after his treacherous conduct
to his brother-in-arms, Leopold of Austria, when out hunting, met
with a severe injury to his right leg—surgery was not then what
it is now—the limb mortified, and it was agreed on all hands
that nothing could save the Prince's life but amputation. But who
was to do it? No one would venture—when Leopold himself proposed that a sharp hatchet should be laid across his limb, and that,
at his word of command, it should be struck with a ponderous mallet,
when it was expected that the limb would be severed. The operation
succeeded so far as the cutting went, but the bystanders were unable

At last, however, came one fatal morning, the 6th of April, 1667, when Ragusa was all but annihilated by an earthquake. In a few moments all the principal edifices in the town were laid low, including the Cathedral of King Richard, and upwards of six thousand inhabitants, more than one-fifth of the entire population were buried in the ruins. There was not a family in the whole city which had not one or more to mourn for. Several of my ancestors perished, and among others a lineal ancestor of my mother, Simone Ghetaldi, then Rettore of the Republic; he and several senators were assembled in the Council Chamber, and about to receive the visit of a Dutch Embassy (which had stopped at Ragusa on its way to Constantinople, to which court it was accredited) when they were all engulphed; not one escaped, and it is supposed that at that spot the earth must have opened and closed over them again. The Archbishop barely escaped with his life by jumping out of a window as the floors of his palace were giving way beneath him, and more than nine-tenths of the clergy perished.

to staunch the blood, and the Prince bled to death—a fitting retribu_ tion for his treachery.

We preserve in our family a manuscript which gives an accurate account of this terrible catastrophe; as a youngster, I was often made to copy it out, and I therefore know it almost off by heart. It tells how the morning of the 6th of April, 1667, broke calm and bright, and that the atmosphere was still and serene, without anything to indicate the approaching danger, when suddenly, without any premonitory sound, about two hours after sunrise, while most of the inhabitants were still in their houses, or in the churches hearing early mass, the earth shook so violently that in a few minutes the whole town was in ruins, with the exception of the fortress, and a few other buildings, the walls of which were enormously thick. In addition to the destruction caused by falling houses, large rocks came toppling down, detached from the mountain, which, as you see, apparently overhangs the city. This added greatly to the terror and devastation. So far as we know there was but *one shock*, and it lasted only a few seconds; but no where and at no time was so much damage done thus instantaneously.

"Many harrowing scenes were recounted, but

perhaps the most terrible of all was that of a school of boys which was swallowed up beneath the ruins. All the unfortunate lads perished, most of them by a miserable lingering death, and for days their moans and cries for help and water could be heard by their distracted friends, without the possibility of giving them any relief. One would have thought this a sufficient visitation for poor Ragusa, but calamities never come singly. A fire broke out on the same day, and towards evening a strong wind arose and fanned the flames, thus increasing the conflagration beyond the power of control. Night came on, and the whole side of the mountains was illuminated by the flames of the burning city. Then the wild mountaineers, the Morlacchi, came down in swarms to pilfer and snatch whatever they could from the universal wreck. The scenes then enacted defied all powers of description. The fires were burning with exceptional brightness and fury, in consequence of the conflagration having reached the stores of oil, tallow and tar accumulated in the Arsenal and elsewhere. Groups of Morlacchi, undeterred by the crumbling walls and the scorching rafters, could be seen flitting about among ruins regardless of the danger! Occasionally some such group having ventured too far, would disappear with a fearful scream into some yawning gulf; while in another spot two parties of the same plunderers might be seen in deadly conflict, fighting with their long straight knives over their unlawful booty. It was a fearful night.

" But all this is ancient history; there is another tragic episode connected with Lachroma. Another calamity is brought to our minds when we look upon its shores. Poor Prince Maximilian!—alas! alas! he was a good and kind man,—and that noble unfortunate Princess Charlotte! I had the honour of being in their company more than once, both in Europe and Mexico; they were so good, so affable, so happy, till in an evil hour they allowed themselves to be led away by ambition. The Prince seemed all along to have had a presentiment of evil. I was told by one who was present, that nothing could be more melancholy than his departure from Miramar, and the leave-taking when he was waited on by a deputation from Trieste was the most painful scene he ever witnessed. The Prince was completely overcome, and fairly broke down on this occasion. After his assassination the island was sold, and now I hear it is for sale again."

The good old Monk was silent for a few minutes, and then gently putting his hand on my shoulder, he said,

"You are English, *non è vero?* You are not American? I would not say a hurtful word to mortal, but I cannot help thinking that the President of the United States was nearly as much to blame as the Mexican savage for the murder of Maximilian; one word from the United States' President would have saved the Emperor's life."

"But what about the French Emperor?" I asked; "he who got the poor Prince into the scrape, and then left him to get out of it as best he could?"

"Ah; true—true," repeated the Monk. "*e quell' altro birbaccione di Bazaine!* Ah! Providence will overtake them all. But look, see how beautiful Ragusa is, how picturesque! Although I am only a poor Capuchin monk, I feel proud of my native city—*che mi son Raguséo!*" he exclaimed, breaking out into his native Venetian dialect. "Though most of my life has been spent far away in foreign missions, I still cling with fondness to my native shores, and feel thankful, most thankful," he repeated, bending his head, "that it has pleased His Holiness and our General to order me back here again at last."

CHAPTER IX.

 FELT an unusual degree of regret, thinking I should so soon lose the company of Padre Anselmo; we had come all the way together from Trieste, and had spent many pleasant hours in genial conversation, flavoured from time to time with spicy, sharp, but good-humoured polemics, during which the Padre never lost his temper, and I had not always the best of the argument.

He was a very remarkable man, of an ancient

noble Ragusan family, evidently pious, yet wonderfully large-minded. I shall always remember with pleasure the conversations we had together on the deck of the 'San Carlo,' by the bright Italian moonlight, on those deep, smooth waters of the Adriatic that sparkled with phosphorescence at every stroke of the paddle-wheel. He was aware I was a Protestant, and though he had been a missionary for many years he knew how to avoid polemics whenever it was fit. He had been in South America and in North America; in the plains of the Amazon and the Orinoco, and among the Sierras of Mexico.

I asked him about his success among the Indians, and after reflecting for a little he gave me a most interesting account of his life's labours among them. I carefully noted down each night in my diary, after we had parted, the principal headings of his narrative, and some day I may give to the public an account of the labours, trials, and sufferings of this good and conscientious monk.

In answer to my question as to the amount of success he had obtained during his long intercourse with American Indians, he said,

"There is a most extraordinary difference in intelligence between the different tribes, even among those living close together; some are wonderfully more intelligent than others, and, strange to say, I found them better the farther they were removed from the influence of civilization. A great deal might be made of them were it not for the evil influence of the traders who come among them— the most pernicious of whom I invariably found were those coming from the United States. These traders, pioneers of civilization—as they called themselves — were almost invariably men without any religion or principle; awful blasphemers, their oaths were too terrific! They generally consisted of the veriest scum and offscourings of commercial cities; they showed the poor savages the very worst examples, for fair trading was unknown to them, and lying, overreaching, and brow-beating were their chief characteristics, while of drunkenness and unblushing debauchery they were terrible examples. I was once asked by a chief why we came so far to teach them, and left our own people un- taught."

Padre Anselmo also told me that some of the

natives had some idea of the Divinity, and were very teachable, not like the Negroes of the West Coast of Africa among whom he had laboured a short time. He contrasted the capabilities of both races, and shaking his head, added,

"I fear it will take hundreds of centuries of incessant teaching, and that more by example than by word of mouth, before any good will come from missions among the Negroes; they seem utterly incapable of understanding any of the attributes of God. They look upon him invariably as one to be feared, and propitiated by gifts and sacrifices, so that he may be induced, if possible, to do them no harm."

A chief came to him one night by stealth, " but not like Nicodemus," as the worthy Monk added; he brought various presents to the mission, some of considerable value, consisting of native rings of twisted gold. He whispered under his breath to the Monk,

"You white man know everything, and you say your God rules everything. Tell me where I can find him, that I may kill him! he is a bad god—

he has killed my favourite wife, and now I must kill him !"

The Negro was foaming at the mouth from impotent rage, and his fearful language, together with the rolling of his eyes and the contortions of his body, impressed the Monk at first with the idea that he was an impersonation of the Evil One. Yet this chief had till then been the most promising of all those natives on whom he had been wasting his time, his patience, and his doctrine. In vain the Missionary tried to reason with the demoniac chief; his words made no impression, and the savage, failing to discover from the Monk the where-abouts of the white man's God, returned to his village, where he burned his own national fetish, and then cut off the heads of half-a-dozen wretches, having first charged them with messages to be delivered to his wife in dead-man's-land !

One evening Padre Anselmo and I, after making ourselves snug on a pile of sacks near the binnacle, were talking about missionary work, when he spoke to me about our Protestant missions, and asked me many questions concerning them.

"You work your missions differently from the way we do ours; you pay your missionaries well, and even allow them, I have been told, to trade at times, and to buy and sell and follow different callings. I have also heard that you send missionaries abroad without any particular regard to their capabilities, for instance as to their knowledge of the language of the country they are sent to. Now all our missionaries are strictly prepared for the country where they are intended to labour, and are not sent out until they have acquired a good knowledge of the language of that country. How do you find your system to work? Have you had much success in the East Indies during the hundred years you have had the opportunity of working in them?"

I imagined I could detect something of a smile playing about the corners of his mouth as he made these remarks, and just as I was about to reply, a scene came to my mind of which I had read or heard an account somewhere, of an English missionary addressing an Arab audience in Tangier through the medium of a Gibraltar Jew, for the missionary was utterly innocent of any language but his own London English, and my innate appreciation* of the ridiculous so overcame my sense of what was proper and decorous that I laughed myself nearly into fits.* However,

---

* The story, as well as I remember it, was as follows :—A probably well-meaning but decidedly weak-minded Protestant, bent on missionary work, arrived one day at Tangier. He had never been in the East, and did not know a word of Arabic. He was determined, however, to improve the opportunity by letting in a ray of Gospel truth into the minds of the benighted Mussulmans. That he did not know a word of their native language was no obstacle to this energetic missionary, he would employ an interpreter. Having found one in the person of a 'Gibraltar Jew,' he explained to him what he wanted; the bargain was soon struck, and the Jew undertook, for a consideration, to interpret for him on the next market day. He, however, advised the missionary to have a certain quantity of tobacco and coffee ready to treat the assembled hearers, as it was always customary to do so in that country whenever an important meeting was held—to which the missionary at once consented. The fact of the danger he would be running into himself, dragging his interpreter after him, from telling the most bigoted perhaps of all Mussulmans, that their religion was false, and their Prophet an emissary of the Evil One, never once entered into his head ; but, fortunately for them both, the Jew had more brain than his employer. Market-day came, and the

having recovered my equanimity, I replied, "I did not know very much about the matter; but I had always heard that, generally speaking, the native Christians were the greatest blackguards in India, the least objectionable being certainly the Goanese Catholics," at which the good old monk seemed highly pleased.

His ideas of missionary work were peculiar and interesting. "We should always," he said "treat

Jew had bespoke, in a couple of cafés, a large supply of coffee. The town and country people having been informed that an " Effendi Engleez" would make a great speech to them, they collected in large numbers in the market-place, where they squatted down round a hogshead, on which the missionary was mounted. He at once began in the usual terms—his religion was the only true one, and all those who differed from him went straight down head foremost into Gehenna, which the wise Jew translated thus : " The Effendi has come all the way from England to get cured ; he is mad, but quite harmless, and if you only have patience, you will get plenty of coffee." And so the missionary went on ringing the changes on his subject, whilst the wiser Jew rang the changes on his ; which, however, always ended in the stereotyped, " and you'll get plenty of coffee." The report, probably made to head-quarters by that enterprising missionary, would be interesting to read, especially by the light thrown upon it by the interpreter ; and how many more missionary efforts might prove equally distressing could we but have together with the sermon the running commentary of a non-interested looker-on.

savages and the utterly uneducated, whether at home or abroad, who are scarcely better than savages, like little children, like very little children in intelligence, yet endowed with the passions and vices of grown up men. One should therefore, if possible, never try to teach them things beyond their understanding, but make their practical civilization proceed *pari passu* with their religious training—instilling morality before preaching doctrine and dogma, both teachings being backed up by unexceptionable example. "These are not my own ideas," added Padre Anselmo, "they are the precepts of the wonderful man who preceded me in the Amazon Mission, the present Pontiff, His Holiness Pope Pius IX., whose equal will never again occupy the chair of St. Peter."

"What! was the Pope ever a missionary?" I asked with astonishment. I knew he had been a soldier, and had been even assured that in his early days he was initiated a Freemason in a Lodge in Sicily; there was nothing very extraordinary in his having been a missionary, but I had never heard of it before, and was therefore taken by surprise.

" Indeed he was," replied Padre Anselmo, " and a very zealous and hard-working missionary, whose memory is reverenced to this day, among many a wild tribe on the banks of the Amazon."

Then we began to talk politics, that is to say I talked, the Monk only listened, till musingly I said, " I wonder who will succeed him in the Chair of St. Peter?"

" Whoever he may be," replied the Monk, " he will have a difficult task coming after such a man."

" Have you been lately at Rome?" said I.

" I was there two months age," he replied.

" What then do you think of Cardinal P——? do you know him?"

The Monk fixed his eyes on me for a moment, as if he would have read my most inmost thoughts, and then speaking very slowly, said:

" That Sicilian Monk has long been aiming at the Tiara; he lives within himself, has no confidant, no intimate friend, has no talents, only plenty of doggedness, *vorrebbe Papeggiare*, but no, never will he occupy the Pontifical chair, never!"

and the Monk, for a minute looked me full in the face.

We were now getting quite close to the town, which is built on the narrow strip of land that lies between the Adriatic and the Dalmatian mountains, that here rise up almost perpendicularly behind it. The morning mists were clearing off, and the hazy outlines of the towers and ramparts, the cupolas and steeples, together with the bright colouring of the sails of the felucas and trabaccoli gliding out of the harbour, threading their way through the many islands scattered outside it, formed a picture that might be realized by a painter but of which I will not attempt the description.

We were now fairly in the port of Gravosa, and the steamer was surrounded by native boats conveying eager candidates for the privilege of carrying ourselves and luggage to the shore. The real port is at Ragusa itself, sheltered and protected by the ancient bastions and towers of the city, but, though amply deep enough for its ancient galleys, and for those argosies (so named after this very city of Ragusa) which in ancient times monopolized with

Venice the commerce of the world, it is not now large enough or deep enough to accommodate our modern practical, though inelegant fire-ships. It has consequently been abandoned for the port of Gravosa, which is not only large, safe, and commodious, but also exquisitely beautiful, though inconveniently distant, being nearly a mile from the city. An excellent road, however, originally made by the French and subsequently improved by the Austrians, communicates between the two places, and numerous small carriages drawn by one or two horses are constantly in readiness to convey for a trifle those who do not wish to walk to Ragusa.

The two monks and I were soon on shore, and there I reluctantly parted with them; they went on foot towards their convent, while I took a small one-horse carriage and started off to the city.

Away we went at full gallop skirting the harbour, till the rising ground at the end of the little valley compelled our lively little horse to a slower rate of progression. We soon however topped the hill, when we again came in view of the sea on our right hand, while on our left were numbers of villas peeping out through masses of oleanders and gigantic aloes, whose flower stems, like colossal candelabra, fifteen to twenty feet in height, gave a peculiarly exotic character to the scene. Many of these villas were in ruins, and others more or less damaged, still bearing evidence of the French occupation at the beginning of this century, and of their expulsion by the Russian and Montenegrin troops.

Ragusa was now fairly again in sight, and a noble city it is, and how picturesque! so far as its greatness is concerned, Ragusa is now but the shadow of what it was in bygone days. Its political importance has faded away—its commercial supremacy is a thing of the past; but its local beauty, its domes, its campaniles, its lofty cut-stone palaces, its churches and public buildings, its exquisitely clean streets, its balmy air, its azure sea and its pleasant society—all these are things real and of the present. But Ragusa is not a place to be described, it must be seen and studied to be appreciated. See it from the land, or from the sea—wander through its narrow, quaint, artistic streets, ramble round its walls and ramparts, and you will find it from every point of view a most remarkable place.

This grand old city, into which neither horse nor carriage is ever allowed to enter, was founded about the beginning of the seventh century, not very long after the foundation of Venice. Both cities were Republics, rivals in commerce and in the arts, and their people were incessantly at war with one another. But though Venice, by degrees, was able to subdue and include in her grasp almost the entire Eastern coast of the Adriatic, she never succeeded, either by cajolery or brute force, in conquering the Ragusans, who maintained their freedom till 1806; when, after existing as an independent State for upwards of a thousand years, during which time it had remained as an advanced post of European civilization on the borders of wild Bosnia and fierce Albania, it fell with Venice, Genoa, and the other free communities of Europe which Napoleon I. wiped off the map of the world.

All down the coast of the Adriatic may be seen the winged Lion of St. Mark, wherever the encroaching ambition of the Venetians enabled them to establish themselves; but in Ragusa you will seek that grim Venetian effigy in vain. Ragusa never was conquered by her great rival!

The carrettella came spinning, at the rate of a hunt, down the hill, at the bottom of which is the entrance to Ragusa, and turning sharp round at a speed that threatened to upset us bag and baggage into the middle of the road, pulled up suddenly on the right, where a very primitive hotel offers the only prospect of refreshment to the chance traveller in those parts; though, for such as intend remaining some little time, good accommodation can be obtained within the city. The hotel is most picturesquely situated on the very edge of the sea, opposite to the fortifications " *di mare*," and has in front a considerable plantation of beautiful Paolonias, then in full blossom; on the opposite side is the café, where of a Summer's evening congregate the rank and fashion of Ragusa to enjoy their ices and lemonade, and listen to the excellent band of the Austrian regiment quartered there, and whatever gossip, scandalous or otherwise, that may be buzzing about. And very enjoyable it must be! fine climate, pleasant society, lovely scenery, easy access to the rest of Europe, either East or West, and cheap living—what more could be desired? I would not ask for more.

CHAPTER X.

IT has always been a source of much astonishment to me, seeing the facility with which these parts can be reached from Trieste, that so few of the ubiquitous English—indeed, 1 might say none of them,—ever visit them, or any of the other many beautiful and interesting localities which crowd the Eastern shores of the Adriatic. I really believe

those countries are not visited because they are
in a certain sense unknown. I trust, however, that
some of my readers who may perchance be tired
of those hackneyed tours which, year after year,
are undertaken by the travelling multitudes, will
try a venture some day in Dalmatia.

Starting from Trieste in one of the many coasting
steamers which trade to Corfù, stopping at every
place on the Eastern shores of the Adriatic from
Capo d'Istria downwards, and making excursions
from each into the interior, anyone fond of everything beautiful and picturesque, whether in nature
or in art, would have the most delightful trip
imaginable; and if getting out at Cattaro he will
scale those wonderful mountains which seem ever
on the point of toppling over on that devoted city,
and penetrate into Montenegro, coming back to the
Adriatic by the Lake of Scutari (or Skodra as it
ought to be called) in Northern Albania, he will
have made an excursion in the heart of Europe,
within seven days from London, and in the short
space of five weeks, which for beauty of country,
wildness of scenery, novelty of life, and magnificence of native costumes cannot be equalled from

Spain to the Caucasus, or from Norway to the Lebanon !

Having made my adieux to Mr. Paton, our Consul at Ragusa, to whom as well as to Persich Effendi, the Ottoman Consul, I was largely indebted for much kind advice, as well as for a personal introduction to Mr. Yonin, Russian Consul at Ragusa, who subsequently at Cattaro and at Cettigne proved a kind friend and most valuable and charming companion, I returned on board and was soon steering south again. We steamed quite close inland, and had an excellent view of the ancient fortifications of Ragusa and its old harbour, only frequented at present by the felucas and trabaccoli which carry on the coasting trade of the country.

We also passed close to the island of Lachroma. The Russian Consul, Mr. Yonin, told me it was for sale and would probably go cheap. I can't conceive a spot on earth where a man tired of the bustle of life and the feverish excitement and turmoil of cities could more delightfully spend the remainder of his days. There is a fairly good house on the island, which is itself beautifully wooded and laid-out. It is sufficiently near to Ragusa to enable one to obtain everything one could require from that city, it is right in the gangway of all the steamers going up and down the Adriatic, within five days of London, and with such a number of communications with the outer world that it would be seclusion only as long as one wished it to be so.

As to the climate, none more beautiful could be desired—sufficiently warm to grow figs, grapes, and oranges, yet daily tempered in Summer by the delicious sea-breeze of the Adriatic, which prevents the heat from ever being oppressive, while of Winter there is barely the name—the thermometer seldom going down to frost.

The sea teems with fish of the most delicious kinds, some of which are totally unknown among us; the dentale coronato, for instance, the true sardine, and the rosy mullet, the woodcock of the sea, which here grows to an immense size—while from the mainland one can always obtain at wonderfully low prices abundance of small mountain mutton, poultry, and game.

I never was in any place that took my fancy like

Ragusa and Lachroma—so lovely, so picturesque, so secluded, and yet so accessible!

Since my return to England I have heard with deep regret of the loss we have sustained by the death of A. A. Paton, Esq., our Consul-General at Ragusa. The country has to regret in him an able and industrious servant, while literature has to mourn for one of its most gifted votaries, as his works on Egypt, Servia, and the Adriatic will amply attest; but only those who had the pleasure of his acquaintance can at all venture to measure the loss which his death must be in his own family circle!

Now the bell rings, and Giovanni bustles up and down the deck, intimating, "*che'l pranzo ze pronto,*" so down we all plunged into the saloon, where a good dinner, as usual, welcomed us.

As the coast is uninteresting, besides which I don't want to go on deck at present, I may as well tell you of what our Italian dinner consisted. We first had an excellent Julienne soup, with abundance of grated Parmesan for such as appreciated it; next was served the "*fritto,*" according to old Italian custom, which always enumerates the following dishes, to succeed each other in an orthodox dinner:—minestra, fritto, lesso, umido, arrosto, dolce, frutta, and, when in season, slices of melon, or fresh figs, served up immediately after the soup, to be eaten with thin slices of raw ham or Bologna sausage. Figs being in season they were not wanting, so conforming to the usage of the country I ate some with raw Bologna sausage, and learnt fully to appreciate the strange compound, which I afterwards always indulged in whenever I had a chance.

The *fritto* was delicious (assuredly nowhere else can they fry as in Italy); it consisted of zucchettine and fiori, *i.e.*, young unexpanded gourd flowers and very young gourds not bigger than an egg, cut in thin slices, dipped in the thinnest of batter and fried quite crisp and golden brown, and served dry without a particle of grease. Then came a dish of *gnocchi alla Milanese*, a superb dish, but difficult to explain; imagine the ingredients of a colossal *vol-au-vent à la financière*, replete with livers, cocks' combs, unborn eggs, &c., &c., surrounded by a bastion of a peculiar preparation, made of maize-flour, and the whole bathed in tomato sauce and sprinkled right over with grated Parmesan, "*proprio da far riavere i morti*," as the *chef* exclaimed to me after dinner, when, handing him a cigar, I complimented him on his *gnocchi*. Then came the *arrosto* which consisted of veal and fowls, and after that a splendid *piatto dolce* of stewed peaches in an artistic cage of caramel sugar, ornamented with strange devices of most delicious marzapane.

Having slowly worked our way through this sumptuous repast, we went on deck, where coffee was served with its usual accompaniment of Maraschino, both sweetened and unsweetened, together with the inevitable smoke, which contrary to reason, as one would think, is even more comforting in hot countries like the Levant, than it is in cold damp regions like Holland.

I have a dim recollection of the captain tapping me on the shoulder and telling me something about Regusa Vecchia and Epidaurus as we were steaming down the coast; but I was in too dreamy a state to pay much attention to him at the time, and as I knew the coast was uninteresting, I told him to call me as soon as we should come in sight of the Bocche and Castelnuovo, and dozed away again.

I afterwards learnt that this Epidaurus, about which I was rather fretting for having refused to stir from my siesta to look at it, was really not worth seeing, though an ancient city, having been founded by a Greek colony somewhere about 700 years B.C., more or less; but all its antiquities had been removed long ago.

It was between three and four in the afternoon when I awoke of my own accord, thus anticipating the captain, who was just coming to tell me that we were about entering the canal of Cattaro, as it is called, but which to our ear is far better described by the name of Fjord of Cattaro. It is to all intents and purposes a Fjord, being an arm of the sea running up for eighteen miles into land, between high precipitous cliffs; and if there is not a glacier at the end of it, but only a quaint Dalmatian town with the most picturesque fort and fortifications in the world, it does not alter the character of the inlet.

The entrance to this Fjord, called " le Bocche di Cattaro," is guarded on the right by the Fort of

Castelnuovo, and on the left is bounded by a narrow strip of Turkish territory, a portion of Herzegovina, which here comes down to the Adriatic, separating the Circolo of Ragusa from that of Cattaro. By some strange political arrangement, or oversight more probably, another narrow strip of Turkish territory comes down to the Adriatic on the north of Ragusa, completely isolating that ancient Republic which finds itself thus entirely surrounded by Ottoman territory on three sides, while on the fourth it is bounded by the Adriatic.

The country about the entrance of the Bocche di Cattaro is fine, well wooded and planted with olive trees, through which can be seen numerous habitations, while many of the rugged heights are crowned with semi-fortified churches, which served as places of refuge to the women and children in troublous times.

Proceeding onwards, the scene varies and the trees lessen in numbers, though the landscape loses nothing of its beauty, as by the constant windings of the Fjord the changes are continuous and rapid, and the many villages built on the edge of the water, and sharply reflected in it, add one more charm to the picture. At one point the Fjord is barely half a mile across, when suddenly it expands into a lake of many miles in circumference, where all the navies of the world could lie in safety. But now the scene changes again and the Fjord becomes a narrow tortuous channel, bounded on either side by naked rocky cliffs. Like the rest of the coast of Dalmatia it is, however, very beautiful. About half way between Castelnuovo and Cattaro, the Fjord expands and divides right and left forming two bays, that of Risano to the left, and that of Cattaro to the right; while in front rise the almost perpendicular crags of Montenegro, at the foot of which, with barely room to build on, so near does the mountain come to the edge of the water, stands the town of Perasto with the ancient fort of Santa Croce just above it.

This place must have been of considerable importance within late years, still I never saw such a picture of poverty and desolation. The houses are not in ruins, but look dilapidated ; the windows are broken in, the jalousies hanging by one hinge and in pieces, while in many places the roofs are stripped of their tiles. The position of Perasto cannot be surpassed; built on a promontory facing the west, it has the lake-like expansion of the Gulf of Cattaro in front and does not consequently labour under the disadvantage Cattaro suffers from, by having a chain of mountains in front of it to the westward, which deprive it of the sun in Winter before two o'clock in the afternoon. The style of the houses in Perasto shows that not long ago it could boast of an opulent population, which is further exemplified by the fortress built at the expense of the town—by its lofty steeple and by its churches. One in particular caught my eye from the steamer, *it had no façade*, not that it had fallen into ruin, neither had it been shaken down by an earthquake, but was built so; open to the weather with a half cupola something like one of those little roadside shrines dedicated to the Virgin which we meet with constantly in Italy and other Catholic countries, only on a very much larger scale.

I felt quite interested in Perasto, it looked so picturesque, so noble, so poor! One house especially struck my fancy, but the word house

does not convey its appearance, it was what an
Italian would call a palazzo. The entrance was
evidently from a back street, while the side which
faced the water consisted of a *loggia* of many
pilasters and arches, into which opened the rooms
of the ground floor, while above it were tiers
of large and handsome windows. In front of the
loggia was a paved terrace, from which a series
of steps, the whole length of the house, led down
to the water. It was uninhabited and in fact
going rapidly to ruin! I fancied to myself what
a little paradise one could make of it; I saw in
my mind's eye a row of orange trees growing on
that terrace, a yacht moored close into those
steps, and life and bustle in those chambers
where all was now silence and decay. What can
have brought such desolation on Perasto? I
asked several people but I could get no satisfactory
answer! some blamed Austria, some *il commercio;*
I suppose I could have bought the fee simple of that
house in Perasto for a £10 note.

In front of Perasto are two small islands—
San Giorgio and La Madonna. In the church of
La Madonna is to be seen an ancient picture

of the Virgin, attributed as usual to the artistic efforts of the Evangelist Luke, who evidently, from what I have seen of his works of art in different places, was not possessed of much talent in that line. Tradition states that the picture was transported in 1452, by an unknown hand, from Negropont to this rock; and being seen amidst lighted candles by some fishermen, it was removed to the church of Perasto. The next night it returned to the island; and the same action having been repeated three times, it was presumed that the picture preferred remaining there; thus they built a church for it, which no doubt turned out a profitable speculation.

CHAPTER XI.

TURNING our backs now on that branch of the Fjord which leads to Risano, we steamed due south in the direction of Cattaro. Nothing could exceed the wild grandeur of this portion of the Gulf. The right hand shore was now entirely in the shade, while the crags on the left being exposed to the full glare of the afternoon sun showed a play of colours too beautiful to describe. Had these cliffs been clothed with varied foliage interspersed with the rocks, they would have formed a picture unequalled in any other place on the globe.

It was six o'clock when we moored alongside the quay of Cattaro, one of the most picturesque cities of the whole Adriatic, so I had plenty of time to walk about and see the place as well as to make arrangements for my advance into Montenegro on the following day, as I was anxious to proceed at once to Cettigne, in order to be present at the festival of St. Peter, during which a fair is held, to which congregate thousands, not only from Montenegro, but from all the surrounding countries. Thanks, however, to Persich Effendi, the Ottoman Consul at Ragusa, to whom I had brought an introduction from the Ottoman Ambassador at Vienna, I found everything already prepared for my trip. The agent of the Austrian Lloyd at Cattaro, Signor Jackschich to whom I can never feel too much obliged, had already procured for me a guide and two horses, thus saving me all trouble, and allowing so much more time to look about me at Cattaro. As soon as we had obtained *pratique*, the formality of which we carried out regularly at every place we touched, though, in reality, it was a farce, Signor Jackschich came on board, and having introduced himself and told me what he had arranged, placed himself at my disposal for the rest of the evening. We at once went on shore, and traversing the Mall, which lies between the quays and the walls of the city, and which serves as the promenade of the *Bocchesi*, we passed through the principal gate of Cattaro, and entered the precincts of the fortifications.

Here, as in most other cities in Dalmatia, no horse, or vehicle of any kind (except sedan chairs) is allowed to enter. The streets in consequence are beautifully clean, and the piazza, which is paved in squares of alternate coloured marble, is more like the floor of the hall of an Italian palace than anything else. The streets are narrow, as might have been surmised, but there are some very fine old houses, some exquisite bits of art hidden away in nooks and corners which one would have loved to sketch had there been time, half built up porticoes with oleanders peeping over them, and bits of lovely hammered iron work of the Renaissance period. But I had no time, so after making a rapid tour through the little city, we came out on the promenade, as I was anxious to have another view of Cattaro, from the outside, before it became too dark.

My friend Paton does not render half justice to this city in his charming book, " The Highlands and Islands of the Adriatic ;" but he is so in love with Ragusa—and, if truth must be told, so am I —that he has nothing to say for Cattaro ; it is true he saw it in Winter, when it must be a dismal place. But Cattaro, for all that, deserves a visit, and anyone fond of sketching will spend, with profit, several days in and about the place. It is situated at the extreme end of the Fjord of that name, on a very narrow ledge of land at the foot of the most precipitous cliffs facing the west, up which it extends for a short space. It is surrounded by the ancient Venetian walls, bastions and fortifications, and crowned by a fort perched on the very summit of the rock, a thousand feet above the city. Looking at it from below, it seems scarcely balanced on the cliff, and one expects to see it come tumbling down every moment.

The fortifications of the town are connected by crenelated walls with the fort itself on two sides,

thus inclosing a considerable space on the face of
the mountain, something in the shape of a triangle,
of which the town would form the base, and the
fort the apex, which is still garrisoned, and many
a harmless rusty old cannon can be seen peeping
through the embrasures.   Having returned from
the opposite side of the water, where I had gone
the better to see the fortifications, we took a walk
up and down the esplanade between the water and
the walls, to look at the *beau monde* on their boulevard, and then adjourned to the café on the same
esplanade to have some ices *al fresco*, and make
our final arrangements for the following morning.

The public walk at Cattaro is very well laid
out, and the most is made of the very contracted
space at command. Two rows of large trees extend along the walls on each side of the gate, above
which is to be seen, as usual, the Lion of St. Mark.
Not so natural, perhaps, as Edwin Landseer's ani-
mals at the foot of Nelson's column ; but, certainly,
a more dignified beast than the one with straight
tail which until lately kept watch and ward over
Trafalgar Square from the top of Northumberland

House. At the northern end of the Mall is the café, and round about it the grounds are laid out in gardens, where, under the shade of gigantic oleanders and mulberry trees, little round tables, made of enormously thick slabs, resting on short central pillars, for all the world like Brobdingnagian mushrooms, are laid out and surrounded with stools for the accommodation of all comers. The stone of which these round tables are made is powerfully sonorous, and if lightly struck, even with one's knuckles, gives out a beautiful soft tone. If cut into lengths and properly poised, excellent rock harmoniums could be made of it.

Here I fell in again with the Russian Consul, who introduced me to one of the finest specimens of men I ever saw, a Montenegrin chief, by name Pero Pejovich, commandant of the Grahovo (pronounced Graho), who had come from Risano in a boat, and was bound for Montenegro to be present at the Feast. He was dressed in full gala Montenegrin costume, *plus* the Risano jacket of crimson cloth without sleeves, thickly embroidered with gold, and on it the medals and decorations he had gained in battle. At another table were seated, also in full costume, two Montenegrin ladies of a family who had been exiled for political causes, and who were waiting at Cattaro in hopes of obtaining an amnesty which would permit them to return to their homes.

The sun had set, and the short twilight had nearly merged into darkness; the great heat of the day was now tempered by a delicious balmy feeling, as the cooler air from the mountains came down to mingle with that of the lower strata; the musical hum of the many voices, the exquisite Trebigne tobacco in our cigarettes, the delicious coffee, all conspired to make that evening one of the most delightful I ever passed. I got another chair, and stretched my legs on it; the natives stared—no Oriental ever thinks of stretching his legs—the acme of comfort for him is to tuck them under him. I felt supremely happy, and expressed myself so.

" I could live here for ever," I said to Signor Jackschich.

" Nay," rejoined Pero Pejovich, " but wait till it rains, and you will soon wish to run away from

Cattaro. I have known it rain here for six weeks without stopping for a moment."

At this juncture, the band of the Austrian regiment quartered here came on the scene, with the same lamp arrangement I had seen at Pola, and for upwards of an hour played the most delicious music to our intense delight. The Consul now reminded me that we should have to start betimes the following morning, if we wanted to avoid being roasted in the middle of the day on the rocks of Montenegro. But the sense of enjoyment was too great, and I could not bear to break the spell of the hour which I was enjoying to the fullest. That I should have an excuse for delaying a little longer, I began to talk in Italian to a little beggar boy who had quietly been asking me for something the whole evening, not with noisy importunate appeals, but by the eloquent look of about the finest pair of eyes that ever were seen.

" Don't take any notice of the young ruffian," said Signor Jackschich, " he is the plague of the town, and the worry of his father. He won't work, and he is in every mischief that is going."

"But I don't tell lies—neither do I steal," retorted the bold young brat, who could be no more than eight or nine. "It is too hot to work, and as to going home to sleep *la dentro*," he said, pointing over his shoulder with his thumb to the town, "when I can enjoy the cool nights under these trees *al fresco*, I would rather not!"

He spoke excellent Italian, and his manner was dignified and self possessed.

"*Diable!*" said Yonin, "*nous avons ici un philosophe!*"

"Can you speak German or French, little chap?" I said.

"No," he replied in Italian, "*non parlo che Illirico ed Italiano.*"

I gave him coins to the amount of about a franc; but when he saw so much money in the palm of his hand—an amonnt which, to his eyes, seemed perfectly fabulous—his first impulse was to hold it out to me again, thinking I was joking with him; but when I assured him it was *veramente tutto per lui,* he cut three capers in the air, and rushed away to where some other children were, to show his treasures and recount his good fortune. Of all the subjects of the Emperor of Austria, in all his vast dominions, I venture to say that the happiest on that night was that little beggar brat in the secluded little city of Cattaro at the far end of his empire in the extreme point of Dalmatia.

CHAPTER XII.

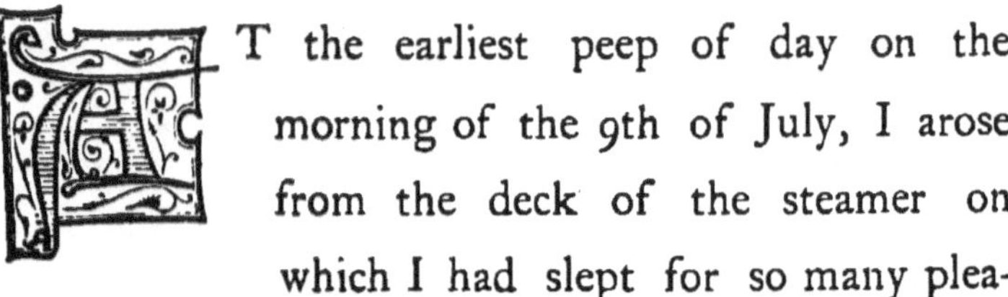T the earliest peep of day on the
morning of the 9th of July, I arose
from the deck of the steamer on
which I had slept for so many plea-
sant nights, notwithstanding its hardness. Thanks
to the kind attention of Giovanni, the steward, a
cup of hot and tolerably good coffee was not
wanting to fortify me against the effects of the
morning air. He wanted me to add a small glass

of maraschino unsweetened "*per scacciar l'aria cattiva*," as he said in his Venetian dialect, but not being addicted to *pegs*, I contented myself with the coffee and a few biscuits.

The faintest tinge of rose showing in the East over the rocks which hang over Cattaro, seeming ever to threaten it with instant ruin, barely enabled me at first to distinguish objects on the mole alongside of which our steamer was moored; but as the light increased I could make out, under the shadow of the trees which form the boulevard and public promenade of the Bocchesi, the stalwart figures of a dozen Montenegrins who had come down from Cettigne to accompany the Russian Consul on his way to the festival of St. Peter, and the court of the illustrious Prince who now so wisely rules those splendid mountain tribes.

Modestly drawn up on one side of them I could see my own portion of the caravan, consisting of only two horses, one to carry myself, the other to carry my luggage, all under the direction of the excellent guide provided for me the day before by the kindness of Signor Jackschich.

Everything was now ready and myself in the

saddle, when the Russian Consul made his appearance, and we finally started just as the dawn was quickening into day.

Skirting by the bastions which defend Cattaro on the sea side, we crossed the bridge that spans the little mountain torrent which here empties itself into the sea, and turning sharply to the right we passed through the open market-place where the Montenegrins come down to sell their farm-produce to the Bocchesi; but who, owing to the somewhat evil name they have unfairly acquired, are never allowed to penetrate into the city unless they first deliver up their arms at the military post outside, just as we do at Aden with the Arabs of the surrounding districts.

Having crossed the market-place, we reached in a few minutes the base of the rocks, and at once commenced ascending that wonderful road zigzagged across the face of the mountain, and known by the name of "*Le scale di Cattaro.*" Here we joined an additional party, also journeying to Cettigne for the festival of St. Peter, and among them was conspicuous the handsome Montenegrin Chieftain, Pero Pejovich, commandant of the

Grahovo, whose pleasant acquaintance we had made the evening before under the mulberry trees of Cattaro.

There was also in the same group a monk, a most picturesque looking individual, but certainly most unclerical-looking. He was dressed in a costume very much resembling the Montenegrin fashion, only of sombre colours, and had his jerkin trimmed with furs instead of embroideries. He wore on his head a sort of black fez, from under which his sable curls fell hanging on his neck, while his full beard, innocent of trimming, flowed amply on his chest. His face was handsome and swarthy, and had a not unkind expression. In figure he was slight, and of medium height. He came from a monastery in the Herzegovina, a province of Turkey in Europe lying co-terminous to Montenegro on its Northern border, and which, strange enough, comes down at one point to the very sea at the opening of the Fjord of Cattaro, thus thrusting itself into and dividing the Austrian sea-board of Dalmatia into two.

What was he coming to Montenegro for? Simply to be inducted abbot of his own monastery, which ceremony by right should have been performed by the Greek Patriarch at Constantinople; but although Herzegovina is subject to the Sultan, yet all the Christian mountaineers of that region, though not Montenegrins by blood, are Montenegrins at heart, and all look to the Metropolitan at Cettigne as their spiritual head, while to the Prince they look up as the only sovereign to whom they owe absolute allegiance.

The abbot elect rode a beautiful, small grey *entero*, wonderfully quick and sure-footed, caparisoned with gorgeous trappings, consisting of a large blue saddle-cloth embroidered with gold, over which lay an immense saddle of crimson velvet studded with large gilt-headed nails. The bridle was of the same Oriental style, while the bit was something to be looked at, both as regards size, ornament and power.

The Abbot sat his *entero*, as if riding at the head of a party of Baschi-Bazouks would be quite as much, if not more to his liking, than leading the chaunts at matins and vespers in his own monastery. There was nothing fierce about his countenance, but there was a sort of "stand and deliver" look about his whole get up, that would have made one feel somewhat anxious had one chanced to meet him *a quattr' occhi* in some lonely pass.

Our caravan consisted in all of about twenty-five persons, as we had been joined by several parties all bent on the same excursion, to partake of the rejoicings at Cettigne. First marched four Montenegrins of the Prince's body-guard, splendid specimens of their race, the shortest over six feet high, with rich ruddy complexions, deeply bronzed by exposure in all weathers, with dark grey or blue eyes, dark brown, almost black hair, cut short, close shaved beard and large moustachios, and fine, open, manly countenances. They wore the national costume of the country, namely, loose baggy blue trousers, made very full and confined under the knee by a strap, below that, their legs were encased in tight-fitting white woollen gaiters, fastened by a row of close-set small metallic buttons all along the back, from the heel to below the knee, while on their feet they wore a peculiar pointed shoe of undressed leather, the upper of which is contrived of numberless small thongs plaited up the middle over the instep, which afford wonderful pliancy and power of grasping to the feet, and are quite characteristic of this region; a sleeveless crimson jacket, and over all the well-known long surtout of fine white cloth, without a collar, fastened round the waist by an enormous silken scarf as much as eighteen feet long, and which supported in front a perfect armoury of weapons. First a yataghan three feet long with richly ornamented sheath and handle, then two highly ornamented Turkish pistols nearly as long, then a poniard, and lastly a special pair of tongs for lifting fire into their smoking pipes, which, excepting when on duty, were never out of their mouths. But as if such an armoury were insufficient, they carried at their sides a formidable-looking, highly curved Turkish sabre, and over their shoulder a long, rakish, Albanian-looking, breech-loading gun. This last they were ever shifting in position, although the favourite mode of carrying it seemed to be across the shoulders, something like the way young ladies at properly conducted schools are made to shoulder their backboards, with their hands hanging over the stock and barrel.

We all followed pell-mell, sometimes in single file, sometimes by twos, according as the inequality of the path or its width, either prevented or admitted of it, while the remainder of the guard brought up the rear. So up we climbed, zigzag after zigzag, some of us above and some of us below until we reach the top of the *scala* where Austrian territory ceases and Montenegro begins.

The sun was now well up above the Eastern horizon, when the sudden cessation of the road gave us notice of our change of territory, and looking round towards the Adriatic to which we mostly had been turning our backs during the ascent, we saw a view that I don't know which would be most difficult, whether to sketch or to describe.

I think we must have been at least three thousand feet above the sea. At any rate, owing to the steepness of the rocks on which we stood, together with the clearness of the atmosphere, the city of Cattaro seemed perpendicularly beneath us, while the coast of Dalmatia, the entire canal of Cattaro with all its windings and the many towns scattered on its coast, the forts at its mouth, and the blue Adriatic beyond, seemed laid out like a map at our feet.

The path, up which we had been toiling ever since we left the town, lay in zigzags before us like a white ribbon stretched out upon the face of the precipice. It reminded me somewhat of the pass of the Gemmi in Switzerland, but was far more beautiful, while the bird's-eye view of the town, with its fortress and its fortifications, was most novel and astonishing. Perched as we were almost perpendicularly over Cattaro, and thus looking right down over their heads, we could see its inhabitants only like black specks moving about its miniature squares and streets, while the old fortress with its crenelated walls and its antiquated bastions, rising out of the bluish haze which hung over the chasm that yawns between the rock on which it is built and the one on which we were standing, made such a picture as Turner wonld have loved to study.

It was one of the most beautiful and extraordinary sights I ever saw, and only lacked the presence of foliage to make it perfect. But total absence of timber is the characteristic of the entire coast of Dalmatia, a fact much to be regretted not only for the loss it is to the country from a picturesque point of view, but principally from the economical aspect of the question—as well managed forests would be of immense value both from the timber they would yield, and the increased humidity they would afford to that arid region, where a sufficient rainfall would increase the fertility, and consequently the revenue more than a hundredfold.

If some of the millions which are yearly wasted by the Austrian Government, as well as by others too, in building ironclads and exploding torpedoes, and in many other equally unreproductive undertakings, were spent on the coast of Dalmatia in planting olive trees on the side of those mountains as far up as they could flourish, then walnut trees, then chestnut trees, and finally oaks and firs, I think I can safely assert that in thirty years the full cost of the first outlay would be repaid, while the benefit to the country at large would be incalculable.

It is not in a book like this that the best modes for bringing about the cultivation of the Dalmatian shores of the Adriatic are to be discussed, but that it could be done and should be done, is undoubted; and not in Dalmatia alone, but also to the east of that country, in the lands beyond the Vellebitch, through Servia, and all that vast tract of country subject now to the impoverishing influence of Turkish mal-administration.

It always makes me sad when I think of those rich countries lying fallow for want of hands to cultivate them, and a good government to encourage industry, and when I see shipload after shipload of hard-working industrious Germans leaving Hamburg, Bremen, and other German ports, risking the perils, the inconveniences, and the expenses of their voluntary exile, traversing thousands of miles of ocean route to reach at last an unknown country, from which it is doubtful if they will ever have a chance of returning to their Fatherland; when those fertile lands of Servia lie at the very threshold of their country, with no sea to intervene, and only a few days of rail and river to go over. But the present state of things cannot continue for ever; and even now promising signs of amendment are not wanting. The monstrous anomaly of some of the richest lands of Christian Europe being still in this nineteenth century under the misrule of barbarous Asiatic hordes, whilst millions of wretched Christian inhabitants are kept in the most abject servitude, must ere long be done away with; and all those countries, Servia, Bosnia, Herzegovina, Roumelia, and all lying between the Danube and the Adriatic must before very long be amalgamated under some one chief. Who the man may be upon whom the noble responsibility may fall of governing this future empire, it is impossible now to conjecture, for the several countries which would go to form this new dominion are still scattered and disorganized; but the great bond of a common language will soon unite them again, when the time comes, and probably that is not distant, for now we do in weeks what our forefathers did in centuries. When that moment shall come, I venture to hope, in the interest of this new country, that one totally unconnected with the present contending clans may assume the direction of affairs.

I know the man but I shall not name him. Handsome in person, brave, courteous, highly educated, and unsullied by any of those Eastern vices which so frequently shock our Western susceptibilities—equally unconnected with either the Kara Georgevich or the Obrenovich parties— his elevation to the throne of Servia would put a stop to that system of hereditary vendetta which seems for the present too deeply rooted in both those clans to permit us to hope in its extinction at least for a time, while it would extend to those countries the benefits of that wise administration which he has already so ably initiated in his own country.   But I must pull up my hobby-horse sharp; he is already in full gallop, and if he once gets the bit between his teeth, he will never check his mad career till he stops at the gates of Stamboul.

CHAPTER XIII.

DURING my stay in Montenegro, I had the honour of several private conversations with the Prince of that interesting country, and I was astonished at the amount of practical knowledge he possessed, and the advanced views he entertained, with regard to commerce, administration, and political economy. But he is cramped up in every way, Montenegro has no outlet, and though his native mountains come so near to the Adriatic that a man could almost spring from them into the sea, still there is everywhere a narrow strip of land between them and that sea, which effectually excludes him from direct commercial or other inter-course with the rest of the world.

This strip of land, in some places only a few yards wide, belongs to Austria and forms part of the Province of Dalmatia. During the reign of Napoleon I. the Principality of Montenegro extended for a short period to the sea shore, and Cattaro was occupied by the Montenegrins till the 14th June, 1814, when it was most unjustly taken away from them again and incorporated with the Austrian Empire by the Congress of Vienna. An act of injustice all the more flagrant, that the Turkish territory was allowed to come down to the sea at the opening of the Gulf of Cattaro, dividing the territory of Ragusa from that of Cattaro, and thus affording the Mahommedan rulers of a Christian land advantages which are denied to the neighbouring Christian Principality.

But whilst I am admiring the scene before me and pondering over the wrongs and the resources of these interesting countries, I must not forget that the sun is every moment getting higher in the heavens, and that it is important to get on with our journey, in order to avoid being out on those arid rocks during the heat of the day.

Our caravan was now in motion again, but the road having almost ceased to exist, we had to proceed more cautiously, picking our way among loose stones and boulders, sometimes following a sort of path, and sometimes climbing up the dried up water-courses of Winter torrents. After another short interval of clambering, we reached a fountain where everyone considered it his duty to dismount and drink, as did also our cattle. When we had refreshed ourselves with copious draughts from that cool spring we again faced up the mountain, but this time on foot, as owing to the steepness and ruggedness of the rocks, it was not deemed advisable to attempt it on horseback.

Except climbing up the cone of Vesuvius, where one generally makes two steps in advance and three steps backwards, I never met anything more trying

than some parts of this ascent into Tchernagora
or the "Black Mountains," as the natives called
this region, and which was rendered by the Venetians into "Montenegro," the name it retains to
this day.

The sun was becoming extremely hot, and I
should have found it considerably difficult to keep
my place, but for the occasional assistance afforded
me by the powerful hand and arm of my Prince
of Mountaineers, Pero Pejovich, who whenever
I came to some rugged impediment which seemed
to tax my energies more than usual, would quickly,
with one hand passed under my arms close below
my shoulder, lift me bodily over it, with his broad
good-humoured face beaming with smiles; and
when I tell you, gentle reader, that I sometimes
weigh *more* but never less than fourteen stone, I
leave you to calculate the strength of my amiable
giant.

We had now topped the worst of our ascent,
and remounting our horses commenced a short descent
to a little plain surrounded by steep, rugged, barren
rocks seemingly the bed of some ancient dried up
lake. At the further extremity of this little plain

could be seen half-a-dozen scattered houses forming the village of Niegosch, the birth-place of the Prince of Montenegro, as well as the cradle of his race, from which they take their patronimic of Petrovich Niegosch.

We rode up straight to the principal house where we were expected and received by a young Petrovich, a cousin of the Prince, a very handsome young fellow, with whom unfortunately I could only have conversation by the help of Pero Pejovich, who speaking Italian as well as Montenegrin, always proved himself a most valuable interpreter.

We made a very short stay here, as we wanted to reach Cettigne before the middle of the day; so having partaken of some excellent coffee, served up with toast and such clotted cream as I never before tasted out of Devonshire, and having admired the gorgeous arms which hung round young Petrovich's room, each of which had some story attached to it, all being trophies taken in battle from the Turks, we mounted our horses, and again plunging into a ravine recommenced the difficult ascent.

After a short but arduous climb, we at lengrh

reached the top of the pass and the highest point between Cattaro and Cettigne. Here a wonderful panorama spread itself out before us—not beautiful, perhaps, but grand in its way. Right, left, and front, nothing could be seen but barren, grey mountain tops—except right in front of us, where at a short distance lay the valley of Cettigne, also apparently the bed of an ancient Alpine lake. Beyond that plain the bleak and rocky mountains closed in again; and beyond them, far in the hazy distance, shining in the noon-day sun, could be seen the glittering lake of Scutari, or more properly of Skodra, in Northern Albania.

A scene like this could scarcely be conceived, such a wilderness of rocks, such a picture of sterility, had never met my eyes. Peak after peak, desolate and barren, rose in every direction, as far as the sight could reach; and as the point on which we stood must have been more than four thousand feet above the sea, the distance we could see in that bright clear atmosphere may be imagined.

The rocks of which those mountains are formed

looked ashy grey in the bright sunlight, except here and there in some of the ravines where a scanty, scrubby vegetation, struggling for existence, offered a precarious subsistence to considerable flocks of small wild goats, herded by still wilder-looking children. These grey rocky masses, when it rains, become of a dark slate colour, nearly black, and hence arose the name of the country, Tcherna-gora.

To account for the presence of such immense quantities of stones in their country, the Montenegrins have a legend which says that after the Creator had made this earth, the Devil was permitted to go and scatter stones all over it. He carried the stones in a bag over his shoulder, but as he passed in his flight over their country, the bag suddenly burst, and thus a greater share of stones fell to their lot than they were fairly entitled to.

I don't know which was the most fatiguing, the climb up to the top of the pass, or the scramble down; I think the latter, and if I did reach the bottom without a fall or a sprained ankle, I owe it all to my excellent fellow-traveller, Pero Pejovich, who kept a sturdy hold of me all through, and saved me, I am sure, from many an ugly tumble.

At last we found ourselves in the little plain of Cettigne, and putting spurs to our small horses cantered over the turf till we reached the first houses of the straggling street which constitutes the capital of one of the most interesting countries in Europe.

The next travellers who visit Cettigne will find there good accommodation in a spacious hotel, which was all but completed before I left; but when I was there, nothing existed in the shape of an inn except a couple of very wretched khans, where it would have been difficult to get rest, owing to the activity of the insect population and the total absence of every accommodation. Thanks to the liberal hospitality of His Highness, I was provided, by his orders, with apartments in the ancient fortified palace of the Vladikas, or Prince-Bishops of Montenegro, to which I was conducted by one of His Highness's aide-de-camps, who had come to meet me. This gentleman had been educated in France, at the Military School of St.

Cyr, spoke French like a Parisian, and was most kind in never allowing me to want for anything. Guessing that I did not know a word of Slave, he had most thoughtfully appointed a man in the town, who could speak a few words of Italian, to attend me during my stay, and to provide me daily with food from a sort of very primitive restaurant in the place.

Having rested a couple of hours after eating an early dinner, according to the fashion of southern countries, I received a visit from Mr. Nico Matanovich, the gentleman alluded to above, and to whom I was indebted for the comfort with which I was installed, who in company with the Russian Consul (who was residing at the new Palace with the Prince), came to propose a walk about the place as soon as the sun should be somewhat nearer to the horizon. Having ordered up coffee, as is always expected in these countries, Mr. Nico Matanovich conveyed to me the agreeable information that His Highness would receive me the following day at eleven o'clock in the morning. In reply, I begged he would present my humble respects to His Highness, and my unbounded thanks for the handsome manner in which I was treated.

The sun being now sufficiently low, we sallied forth to take a turn round the place, and see what was to be seen. But before I leave my quarters, let me try to give some idea of the Vladika's Palace, where I was lodged. This quaint old building consists of a quadrangle of about a hundred and fifty paces* either way, surrounded by a very massive and high wall, pierced by two large roofed-in gateways, one in front and one at the side, and having at each corner a round squat tower with a conical roof, reminding one somewhat of those that surround, at intervals, the Kremlin at Moscow. Running midway from side to side, and dividing this enclosure into about two equal parts is the palace itself, which consists of two stories, the second of which is divided into a series of chambers, each about sixteen feet square and ten feet high, all opening into each other, and communicating also at the back with a wide corridor which goes the whole length of the building. The windows,

---

* I had taken exact measurements, but some of my notes were unfortunately lost—the above measurements are, therefore, only approximative.

of which there are two to each room, look into the front compartment of the quadrangle, while the windows of the corridor look on the back.

The entrance is by a hall door from which one ascends at once to the upper story, by means of a massive wooden staircase formed of solid beams of timber roughly hewn. The lower story has been turned partly into an arsenal, principally filled with ancient weapons taken from the Turks, and partly into a Government school; the upper rooms are occupied at one end by the Archimandrite and some other officials—the rest are untenanted. In the centre of the front court-yard is a deep well of the most delicious water, and so cold that I used it to cool my wine and beer with nearly as much success as if I had been using snow. The back compartment was a kitchen-garden and orchard.

Leaving the old Palace by the side gate which opens upon one of the two streets that constitute the town of Cettigne, we found ourselves opposite to the new Palace lately built by the Prince—the style of which I in no wise admire, though I do not doubt it is comfortable enough inside; but it has no character whatever, and looks insignificant when compared with the old Palace. If the money spent on building the new had been judiciously laid out in adding to the old, a truly fine Palace could have been erected, with all the old characteristics preserved, which the eyes of the people, as well as of travellers, would have had an historical stamp as the abode of all the old Vladikas, those ancient Prince-Bishops—Bishops of the Church Militant—who for many years had valiantly defended their country, their liberty, and their faith against the unceasing attacks of the Infidels.

Opposite this gate, and just midway in the very broad street between the old and the new Palace, stands a large carob tree, with a stone bench of roughly hewn blocks round its trunk, and here in Summer from about nine o'clock every morning the Prince sits f r some hours administering justice. I often watched him with the greatest interest from a window in the old Palace. It was like acting a chapter in the Old Testament—Deborah judging Israel under a palm tree, " between Ramah and Beth-el in Mount Ephraim !" Beyond the " Tree of Justice " one came to the new Palace, a homely structure, as I said before, and of no pretence.

At the gate two sentries of the Prince's body-guard, in full Montenegrin costume, mount guard, and are constantly relieved every hour, their barracks being exactly opposite. The process of relieving guard is very simple—two privates walk out of the barracks with their long breechloaders over their shoulders " *à volonté,*" and take their station on each side of the gateway of the Palace, while the other two walk back into barracks, and that is all.

We now turned our backs on the " Tree of Justice," and walked up the street, which is but short, until we came to the main street which crosses it at right angles. This main street is not paved, but is wide, and the houses on each side, though seemingly poor and wretched in the extreme in our eyes, are, most probably, comfortable enough in theirs; and as they do not even possess a word in their language to denote " comfort," what we would consider such, would, perhaps, be only considered by them an uneasy restraint.

Turning now to the right we walked to the end of the street, where is the new hotel with the post and telegraph office. The hotel, as I previously said, was not yet opened, though the building was completed, and when supplied with beds, tables, and chairs will be a very creditable affair, incomparably better than any hotel in Dalmatia. Near the hotel, a little to the left, is another modern institution, evincing in no small degree the enlightened anxiety of the Prince for the advancement of his country. It is a *Pensionnat de demoiselles* for the education of the daughters of the better classes, both of Montenegro and the surrounding countries ; it can accommodate forty pupils, and is superintended by a charming and highly accomplished Russian lady, assisted by efficient governesses. The charge being very small, only £20 per annum, it must be largely subsidized by His Highness.

Being vacation time, I had not the satisfaction of seeing any of the boarders, much to the regret of Mademoiselle Pakievitch, who kindly showed me all over the institution, which was admirably neat and clean. She was anxious that I should have heard some of the pupils speak English and French. " I think you would have been both pleased and surprised," said she. The majority spoke Illyrian, Russian and German, while several were proficient in addition with both English and French, and one with Albanian also. The institution is under the special patronage of the Empress of Russia, who takes the greatest interest in it, and constantly sends presents to it.

Keeping now a little to the right, and following the path which leads to the town of Rieka, we soon came to the foot of the crags which on that side close in with an impassable barrier the little plain of Cettigne. We now turned sharp round and set our faces towards the town, as the lengthening shadows warned us that the sun was already setting behind the mountains which we had traversed in the morning. The smooth plain covered with short grass was delightful to walk over, though one had to be careful of one's steps owing to the many wells with which it is dotted for the purpose of getting water for the cattle, and which, quite level with the ground and without the semblance of a parapet, might have swallowed one up before one would have had time to see them.

Right before us, standing a little to the left and

just beyond the old palace, could be seen in the distance the ancient monastery which in old times used to be occupied by the Archimandrite, in the days when the Vladika used to inhabit the palace; but now that Church and State are separated, it is occupied by Monsignor Roganovitch, the Metropolitan of Montenegro.

Just above it, perched upon a rock and standing out in bold relief against the glowing sky, could be seen the old tower of Cettigne, an ancient piece of masonry which until three or four years ago used to be constantly decorated with the heads of Turks killed and decapitated in their several skirmishes and forays. This barbarous custom has now been abandoned, never to be resumed again it is to be hoped, and the present Prince, further to turn away the thoughts of the natives from the barbarous habit of their forefathers, has caused a belfry to be erected on the top of the tower wherein is placed a large bell, which is only rung in cases of great alarm to gather the tribes. The bell is very heavy, and much ingenuity and labour were required to transport it on men's backs from Cattaro to Cettigne.

By the time we got back to the Palace it was dark, so wishing good night to my kind friends I made a frugal supper and went to bed.

CHAPTER XIV.

INSECT POWDER OF MONTENEGRO—DESCRIPTION OF THE MO-
NASTERY—ENCAMPMENTS—FESTIVAL OF ST. PETER—A SAINT
BY THE WILL OF THE PEOPLE — PICTURESQUE SCENE —
BOSNIAN CAFÉ—THE NATIONAL INSTRUMENT—A TRAVELLED
DALMATIAN—TALL MONTENEGRINS.

AWOKE early the next morning, having slept most luxuriously on a spring mattress and totally unmolested by fleas, thanks to the ample supply of flea-powder thoughtfully strewn by my attendant, between the mattress and the under-sheet.

The insect powder of Montenegro is celebrated, you must know, in Eastern and Southern Europe, and I can vouch for its excellence. It consists simply in the small dried flower of some species of Pyrethrum, which when wanted for use is ground in a coffee-mill and strewed about the bed. The plant is found abundantly all over Montenegro, and owes its greater virtue to the fact of being grown in very arid soil, untempered by the slightest moisture, and exposed to scorching suns—everything about it therefore is in the most concentrated form, and hence its efficacy; it is a very considerable article of commerce, and is largely exported to Russia and the Levant.

It was not therefore due to insect attacks that I was so early disturbed from my slumbers on the following morning; still I was disturbed, and that by the momentarily increasing hum of many voices and general bustle of the thousands who were flocking to Cettigne for the festival which was to take place on the morrow; but the great day of the feast throughout the south of Europe is invariably the day before the feast, " la vigilia del Santo," as the wording goes. The day of the feast itself one confesses, goes to mass, and does the proper; all the fun and the rollicking is generally the day before. So I got up, and pushing open the outside green shutters which secured my windows, I looked into the courtyard of the Palace, and over the walls beyond into the little plain, which was gradually filling with numberless men, women, and children, some on horseback, more on foot, but all gorgeously attired.

The sun was now getting high on the horizon, and the scene before me was becoming more and more animated and interesting. In the open space under my window, within the high enclosure of the Palace wall, men were busy picketing a dozen horses, evidently from the costliness of their trappings belonging to Chiefs and Woyvodes. While under a group of carob trees, in one corner of the enclosure, were spread several rugs on which were sitting cross-legged some of the owners of those quadrupeds, with their clumsy high-backed saddles behind them, passively smoking their chibouks while their attendants busied themselves preparing coffee.

Close on my right and just beyond the old Palace was the monastery, which, owing to the lateness of the hour the evening before, I had been unable to examine. Like the old Palace it is a sort of semi-fortified building, constructed more for safety than for comfort. On the right hand, as the observer looks at it in front, is the church, and next to it a tall, square, and very modern tower erected to the memory of the Vladika Peter, who is buried on the top of a somewhat difficult peak to the south-west of Cettigne and about six miles distant. The body of the monastery comes next, conspicuous by two rows of arched openings placed one over the other, and to the left of them again are the apartments of the Metropolitan. The whole is surrounded by a high wall, enclosing a primitive garden in which are located a large number of beehives, (upwards of a hundred). This wall is pierced by one large gateway, roofed over and secured by a massive door, in front of which is the circular-paved thrashing floor, so characteristic of the East. Every thing about the monastery is of the simplest and rudest construction, and the church is utterly una-dorned, not from choice, I am assured, but from necessity.

In the monastery itself are many shady corners that would well repay a few hours spent in trans-

ferring them to one's portfolio, and just at the
entrance inside the building, is a most extraordinary
chasm in the rock, through which a piercing cold
wind is constantly blowing, coldest when the
weather is hottest; and so intense is the cold in
that opening that it is used in Summer as an
ice-house for the cooling of wine and the preserving
of food. This phenomenon has never been satis-
factorily explained, because it is not only that the
cavity is cold, but a strong sharp cutting wind
rushes out of it. I shall not attempt to account for
it, but will leave it as a problem for sharper wits
than mine to solve.

As the day waxed older the number of arrivals
increased on the plain of Cettigne, till by eight
o'clock in the morning it was dotted all over
with picketed horses and temporary encampments
of all sorts. Having had my simple breakfast of
coffee, milk, and toast without butter—which is
quite unknown there though cream is plentiful—
but accompanied by a good plate of Albanian figs,
I went out with Pero Pejovich, who came to fetch
me to visit the fair. For this festival of St. Peter
offers a double stimulus to the inhabitants of the

surrounding country for a visit to Cettigne — a religious ceremony and a considerable fair. And it may be right for me to observe that this St. Peter, Patron of Montenegro, in whose honour this great gathering annually takes place, is a saint *sui generis*—indeed I was on the point of saying, when I detected and checked myself, that he was a saint *extra palum ecclesiæ;* for he is neither St. Peter the Apostle, nor St. Peter the Martyr, nor St. Peter the Hermit, nor even St. Peter Igneus, who in a fit of zeal for the maintenance of the laws relating to the temporalities of the church, walked through the flames at Settimo in the eleventh century, to establish a case of simony against another Peter, one Peter of Pavia, then Bishop of Florence; nor any other canonical St. Peter I ever heard of, but simply St. Peter of Montenegro, the old Vladika Peter I., Prince-Bishop of Montenegro, not yet canonized by any ecclesiastical authority or other licensing body, as I was assured, but simply a saint in virtue of the will of the people, the Plebiscite of Montenegro, who insisted *autoritate nostra* on having him for their patron saint. He probably deserved to be canonized just as well, and perhaps better than many another saint, and if history tells truth, certainly better than his namesake, the so-called Peter the Martyr, for he wisely, mildly, and virtuously ruled in Montenegro for fifty-three years, viz., from 1777 to 1830, and the mountaineers are fully justified in reverencing his memory.

Passing my arm through that of Pero Pejovich, who seemed to know and be known of everyone, I began my expedition through a crowd of men, women and children, that every moment grew denser and denser. It was the most picturesque scene that could be imagined; all the neighbouring and surrounding countries had sent their contributions to the fair—Bosnians, Servians, Herzegovinians, Morlacks, Dalmatians, Albanians, Roumelians, Turks, Greeks, Croats, Italians, &c.; but conspicuous among them all for height of stature and nobility of countenance were the Montenegrins themselves. I think that, even independent of their costume, I could have always singled them out by their ruddy though sunburnt complexions, grey or blue eyes, and open honest countenances.

We went to a booth where arms were sold, and I was astounded at the number, variety, and richness of the weapons that were not only displayed, but were actually sold. They seemed to me dear. I should have much liked to purchase a handsome yataghan with silver hilt and in a sheath of *repoussé* silver. It was a very handsome weapon, and was made by a celebrated artificer of Skodra, but the price was sixteen Napoleons, which was more than I liked to give, and I suspect I could get one just like it in Tichborne Street for half the money.

From the armourer we went to a tailor's booth, where piles of costumes of different nationalities were exposed for sale; Morlack suits, Albanian suits, and Montenegrin suits, some of cloth and some of velvet, but all more or less embroidered in gold, and some literally overladen with plates of silver gilt. From thence we went to a Bosnian *café* of the most primitive kind; a couple of large blankets stretched over a few poles made a pretence of shelter, and on the ground were a few Turkish rugs on which we squatted, while a very ugly and dirty gipsy-looking woman was boiling coffee outside over a small fire of sticks contrived between two stones; nothing could be more primitive. So we sat and smoked, and in due time drank our coffee, which was simply abominable. I remember it was, though I was not minding it much, being occupied at the time with listening to a man performing on the national instrument, the *guzla* (pronounced goozla), whilst a girl was singing a low, monotonous, plaintive air.

The *guzla* is not an instrument which offers much scope to the performer; it is simply a very primitive fiddle, with only one string, played upon with an equally primitive bow; still it was surprising the amount of harmony the man contrived to scrape out of it. The song, as Pero Pejovich told me, was all about the old story, love and war, while the music, as is almost always the case among barbarous nations, was in a minor key.

Having paid for our coffee and thrown a few paràs to the minstrels, we sallied forth again.

" And now, friend Pero," I said, " I should

like to see some of your Montenegrin beauties. I have seen lots of fine men this morning; but as to the women, friend Pero, they are a caution. I never saw so many ugly ones congregated to-gether."

My conductor smiled, shrugged his shoulders, and looked me in the face; he did not know exactly whether he ought not to be angry. However, his habitual good-humour prevailed, and with a loud laugh, he said:

" *Avete ragione, son brutte come il Demonio.* But wait, only wait till you see the Princess; she is a pure Montenegrina, and beautiful enough for the whole nation." And he spoke truth!

We now wandered away again towards a sort of native inn or khan, where he said we should get some good Vienna beer to wash away the taste of that abominable coffee. As we were passing some booths, where a variety of cheap Manchester goods were being displayed with some English Delft ware of the very commonest description, I was hailed with a " How d'ye do, stranger?" from a dapper, wide-awake-looking little man, who came out and spoke such excellent English that I took

him to be a Briton or an American; but he was
neither; he was a Dalmatian from Sebenico, who
had been a great deal in England and America,
and spoke English as fluently as his native Illyrian.
I had a long chat with him, and asked him how trade
was, and if he was doing well.

"No," he replied; "they don't know what trade
is in these countries, they have too many restrictions;
and yet," said he, " you won't go into the poorest
cabin that you won't find one of these," handing
me a wretched sample of English pottery with a
vile brown pattern on it; "such is their preference
for everything of English make."

Here Pero reminded me of the beer we had to
drink, and that the time was drawing near when I
was to present myself at the Palace for my audience.
So we went off to the khan, where, having refreshed
ourselves with some of Vienna's best, with a lump of
virgin snow in it, I bid my guide good morning,
and returned to the old Palace; when, having
dressed myself, I crossed over to the new one to pay
my respects to the Prince according to the orders
received the day before.

Having penetrated through the outer gate, where

the guards, I thought, looked rather scowlingly on my strange attire—viz., a dark blue frock coat, light grey trousers, and patent leather boots, the whole topped with my Indian quilted helmet— I ascended to the hall door by half a dozen steps, where I was met by the Prince's own henchman, a brother of the Commandant of the Grahovo. He was yet taller than his brother, and must have been at least six feet eight inches. I do not say this quite by guess-work, though I did not actually measure him; but on a subsequent occasion I did measure an immense Montenegrin, and found him six feet seven inches without heels, and the hench-man was decidedly taller than he.

Well, *pour revenir à nos moutons*, I followed my Goliath into the hall, which is small and low, terminating in a double staircase, that bending round from each side joins again in the middle to form but one flight, at the top of which I found myself in a vestibule with two more guards on duty, and from that I was ushered into a fine large and well proportioned room, handsomely furnished in Viennese style, and hung all round with good portraits of the Prince's father, the celebrated

Mirko, the Emperor and Empress of Russia, the Emperor and Empress of Austria, and many others.

Rooms open right and left off this. I was conducted into a smaller room to the right, where, after waiting for only a few seconds, the Prince came in. He addressed me in French, congratulating me on my courage for having ventured so far into his country, not on account of the difficulty of the road, "for all English are good mountaineers," but from the bad name the country has in Europe.

"Don't you know," said he, laughing, "que nous sommes des ogres, et que nous mangeons les enfans; however, you shall try how we cook them if you will dine here to-night at eight."

I thanked His Highness for his kindness, adding that I had never heard of their cannibal propensities, but in any case I should be happy to eat anything His Highness also would eat, and making my bow backed out of the saloon.

I then left my card for the Russian Consul, who was staying at the Palace, and afterwards went to pay the same compliment to Mr. Nico Matanovich, aide-de-camp to the Prince; after which I returned to my quarters, to convert into a luncheon the repast which otherwise would have served for a dinner, but for the hospitality of His Highness.

CHAPTER XV.

I NOW discovered what a terrible nuisance it is to know only three or four languages, especially when one finds oneself in a country the language of which is a complete mystery. The attendant I had, who had been so thoughtfully provided for me by Mr. Matanovich, professed to speak Italian, and he did in fact know a few Italian words, but in his general conversation

with me, as was ˍsubsequently discovered and explained to me by Pero Pejovich, the language in
which he spoke consisted pretty much of the following happy mixture: six-tenths of Montenegrin,
three-tenths of Albanian and Turkish, with one-
tenth Italian! With this polyglot jumble we got
on fairly well, as far as hot water, coffee, pipe,
tobacco, pranzo; and he learned to appreciate
eventually the American word "skedaddle," but
when our necessities required further intercourse,
it was perfectly hopeless — language was utterly
useless, and gesticulation the only chance of making
oneself understood. But he was a willing poor
beggar, and not more dishonest than the majority
of his fellows. He had a wholesome terror of the
Prince's rigorous punishment of theft. "*Niente
ladri in Montenegro,*" he used to say, "*Principe
terrible,*" turning up his eyes and distorting his
countenance to a fearful degree.

Now whilst my attendant is preparing and setting
out my lunch, I may as well entertain my reader
with an account of the customs in war, and mode
of fighting of the Montenegrins, by the pen of
M. Broniewsky, which is so graphic, and accords

so literally with what the Commandant Pero Pejovich related to me at different times, that I cannot think I could do better than transcribe it.

"A Montenegrin is always armed, and carries about during his most peaceful occupation a rifle (many of them now have breechloaders), pistol, or yataghan, and a cartouche-box. The Montenegrins spend their leisure time in firing at a target, and are accustomed to this exercise from their boyish years. Being inured to hardships and privations, they perform without fatigue, and in high spirits, very long and forced marches. They climb the steepest rocks with great facility, and bear with the greatest patience hunger, thirst, and every kind of privation. When the enemy is defeated and retiring, they pursue him with such rapidity that they supply the want of cavalry, which it is impossible to employ in their mountainous country.

"Inhabiting mountains which present, at every step, passes where a handful of brave men may arrest the progress of an army, they are not afraid of a surprise, particularly as they have on their frontier a constant guard, and the whole of their force can be collected within twenty-four hours upon the threatened point. When the enemy is in great force, they burn their villages, devastate their fields, and after having enticed him into the mountains, they surround and attack him in the most desperate manner.

" When the country is in danger, the Montenegrins forget all personal feelings of private advantage and enmity. They obey the orders of their chief, and like gallant Republicans, they consider it a happiness and a grace of God to die in battle. It is in such a case that they appear as real warriors ; but beyond the limits of their country, they are savage barbarians, who destroy everything with fire and sword.

" Their ideas about war are entirely different from those adopted by civilized nations. They cut off the heads of those enemies whom they take with arms in their hands, and spare only those who surrender before the battle. The property they take from the enemy is considered by them as their own, and as a reward of courage. They literally defend themselves to the last extremity; a Montenegrin never craves for mercy; and whenever one of them is severely wounded, and it is impossible to save him from the enemy, his own comrades cut off his head. When at the attack of Clobuk, a little detachment of our troops was obliged to retreat, an officer of stout-make and no longer young fell on the ground from exhaustion. A Montenegrin perceiving it (the Montenegrins were fighting with the Russians against the French) ran immediately to him, and having drawn his yataghan, said 'You are very brave and must wish that I should cut off your head; say a prayer and make a sign of the cross.' The officer horrified at the proposition made an effort to rise, and rejoined his comrades with the assistance of the friendly Montenegrin.

"They consider all those taken by the enemy as killed. They carry out of the battle their wounded comrades on their shoulders; and be it said to their honour they acted in the same manner by our officers and soldiers.

"Like the Circassians, they are constantly making forays in small parties, for the plunder of cattle, and consider such expeditions as feats of chivalry, (just as the Scotch Highlanders one hundred years ago). Being safe in their habitations, where nobody dares to molest them, they continue their depredations with impunity, disregarding the threats of the Divan, and the hatred of their neighbours. Arms, a small loaf of bread, a cheese, some garlic, a little brandy, an old garment, and two pair of sandals, made of raw hide, form all the equipage of a Montenegrin. On the march they do not seek any shelter from rain or cold. In rainy weather, the Montenegrin wraps up his head' in his strooka, lies down on the ground, and sleeps very comfortably. Three or four hours' repose are quite sufficient for his rest, and the remainder of his time is occupied in constant exertion.

" It is impossible to retain them in the reserve; and it seems they cannot calmly bear the view of the enemy. When they have expended all their cartouches, they humbly request every officer they meet with to give them some, and as soon as they have received them, they run headlong into the further line. When there is no enemy in sight, they sing and dance, and go on pillaging, in which we must give them the credit of being perfect masters; although they are not acquainted with the high sounding names of contribution, requisition, forced loan, &c., &c. They call pillage, simply 'pillage,' and have no hesitation in confessing it.

"Their usual manner of fighting is as follows: If they are in great force, they conceal themselves in ravines, and send out only a small number of shooters, who by retreating lead the enemy into the ambush; here, after having surrounded him, they attack him, usually preferring on such occasions swords to fire-arms; because they rely on their personal strength and bravery, in which they generally have the advantage over their enemies. When their numbers are inferior, they choose some advantageous position on high rocks, where pronouncing every kind of abuse against their enemies, they challenge them to combat. Their attacks are mostly made during the night, because their principal system is surprise.

" However small their force may be, they always try to wear out the enemy by constantly harassing him. The best French *voltigeurs* in the advanced posts were always destroyed by them ; and the enemy's generals found it more advantageous to remain under cover of their cannon, of which the Montenegrins were not at all fond. However, they soon became accustomed to them, and supported by our rifles, they bravely mounted the batteries.

"The tactics of Montenegrins are confined to being skilful marksmen . . . . In a pitched battle their movements can be ascertained only by the direction of their standards. They have certain signal cries, which are uttered when they are to join in a compact body for attacking the weaker points of the enemy. As soon as such a signal is given, they rush furiously onwards, break into the squares, and at all events create a deal of disorder in the enemy's ranks. It was a terrible spectacle to see the Montenegrins rushing forward, with heads of slaughtered enemies suspended from their necks and shoulders, and uttering savage yells . . . .

"The Russian commander-in-chief had much difficulty in persuading them not to cut off the heads of their prisoners. He finally succeeded in this (chiefly by paying them a ducat for every prisoner) but what he had more difficulty, with the assistance of the Vladika, in persuading them to do, was to embark for an expedition on board of ship —a thing which they had never done before.

" Notwithstanding that they were treated with the greatest kindness, they proved very troublesome guests. Whenever the captains invited their chiefs to breakfast, they all entered the cabin, and having observed that more dishes were served to the officers than to common sailors, they wanted to have a similar fare. When the Fortress of Curzola was taken the feast of Easter was approaching; they gave the captain no repose, entreating him to return to Cattaro; but when it was explained to them that the vessel could not advance against the wind, they fell into great despondency.

" When at last the ship approached the entrance of Boccha di Cattaro and they caught a sight of their own black mountains, they uttered joycus exclamations, and began to sing and dance. On taking leave they affectionately embraced the captain and the officers, and invited those to whom they had taken a liking to pay them a visit. But when the sailors told them they could not leave the ship without the permission of their superiors, they were much astonished, and said, 'If you like to do a thing, what right has another to forbid you?'"

Does not the foregoing read like a chapter in "Waverley," or in "Rob Roy?" but though it is now a good many years since M. Broniewski wrote the foregoing, the Montenegrin is still much the same, with the exception of cutting off the heads of those killed in battle, which he has given up, principally, I believe, because he has had no fighting of late. But at the period of the last attempted invasion of Montenegro on the Grahovo side, by the Turks in, I think, 1862, heads were cut off as freely as ever, and were liberally paid for by the chieftains ; the only difference was that instead of taking them to Cettigne to hang in festoons upon the round tower at the back of the monastery, they were allowed to rot on the battle-field among the rocks of the Grahovo where scores of them are to be seen lying about to this day.

CHAPTER XVI.

I REGRET more than I can express
having lost some interesting notes of
several conversations I had with the
Commandant Pedro Pejovich on the
subject of the campaign of 1864 (?); all the more
as they were most graphically told me by him, who
had been in the thick of the fight, and carried in
his body, in the shape of severe wounds, proofs

of the active part he had borne in that campaign. One only I partially remember still, sufficiently well to venture to retail.

The Turks, apparently, were attacking the Montenegrins from the Herzegovina in the north of Montenegro. They numbered about twelve thousand men, together with a good force of Artillery; while the Montenegrins collected to oppose them were not more than two thousand; but whilst the Turks were in the plain fully exposed in sight of the Montenegrins, these sturdy mountaineers, finding covert behind each rock and bramble bush, were able to pick off the Turks with considerable effect. Still the disparity of force was too great, and at the end of the second day's fighting, although the Turks had not been able to make any impression on the position held by the Montenegrins, still the number of those killed and wounded bore a very large proportion to their numbers. At sunset the fight being over for the time, and sentries having been posted by the mountaineers as far forward as practicable to watch the Ottoman camp, Prince Mirko, father of the present Prince

of Montenegro, then in command of the Montenegrins, summoned all the chiefs to a brief council
of war, and spoke thus:

" Two days we have been fighting the infidels,
and the only result has been the losses we have
sustained in killed and wounded. Another day of
such fighting will leave us so crippled that the
accursed Turks will walk over us into our homes
and villages. There is but one plan which offers
any hope, but if you adopt it and place faith in
me, I promise you a complete victory before to-
morrow's sun shall gild the tops of yonder
mountains. To-morrow morning, one hour before
daylight, be all ready to follow me, leave behind
your rifles and ammunition, and follow me softly
and stealthily, making no noise; so we shall pass
the Turkish advanced sentries without their noticing
us, and when sufficiently near I will call my cry,
and then let you all rush forward with me, trusting solely to your yataghans, and give no
quarter."

This was carried out to the letter, and succeeded
perfectly. The Turks, never imagining they would
be attacked, kept a bad look-out. The Montene-

grins, led on by the intrepid Mirko, rushed on the Turkish batteries, cutting the gunners' heads off, and having spiked the cannons attacked the remainder of the army with such impetuosity that they fled from the field in the utmost disorder.

This was the last attack of the Turks against Montenegro, and I don't think they will ever try it again. Prince Mirko was dead before my visit to this country. I cannot therefore give any description of him personally, but from all I heard he must have been a very remarkable man in every way. Though small in stature and slight, contrary to the general build of the Montenegrins, who are mostly all very tall and powerful men, he had immense influence over the mountain-tribes; owing to his well known sagacity and his fierce courage, wherever Mirko would lead, the whole of Montenegro would follow. He had the eye of an eagle, and strength of will and determination are portrayed in every line of his face, as I have observed in his portrait which hangs in the Palace of Montenegro, as well as the photograph I have seen of him. But he was wise also; when Prince

Danielo (the predecessor of the present ruler) died by the hand of an assassin at Cattaro, his widow, the Princess Darinka, at once caused the present Prince, Nicholas I. (nephew of the murdered Danielo) to be proclaimed sovereign, passing over his father Mirko, who, owing to the great youth of his son, might have expected and claimed the succession ; but as I said above, Mirko was wise as well as valorous. He knew that from his own warlike tendencies, how much soever he might be acceptable to his own mountaineers, his elevation to be ruler of Tchernagora would be displeasing to most of his neighbours in Austria, Servia, and Turkey. He therefore at once consented to his son's promotion, and generously was the first in Montenegro to do homage to the young Prince.

Up to the year 1850, when Prince Danielo succeeded to the throne of Montenegro, the country had always been ruled by a Prince-Bishop, styled the Vladika. This dignitary, generally, if not always, nominated his own successor in the person of a nephew or some other near relative, who, on the death of the Vladika at once took holy orders and became in his turn Prince-Bishop.

Danielo, not wishing to give up the happiness of home and married life, and also perhaps with the hope of founding a dynasty of his own in Montenegro, which in the course of time might, by extension and the absorption of other principalities, become an important kingdom, repaired to St. Petersburgh on the death of the Vladika Peter II., his uncle, and there obtained the full consent of the Emperor Nicholas to his effecting a division between Church and State. On his return journey to Cettigne he married at Trieste the Princess Darinka, hoping to have founded a line of princes to succeed him. His hopes however were destined to be blighted. Darinka had no children, and after reigning eight years, he was murdered at Cattaro as I have related above.

The young Prince, (Nicholas I.) who had already been betrothed almost in infancy, as is the custom among the upper classes in that country to a relation of his own, daughter of one of the principal Voyvodes in Montenegro, followed his studies under special direction in the Palace of his ancestors; till one day the late Emperor Napoleon III., for reasons of his own, proposed to have the young Prince sent to Paris, there to be educated under his own eye; and the offer having been accepted, a French man-of-war without loss of time steamed into the Gulf of Cattaro and carried away the young Prince, together with two companions of his own age, sons of two of the principal Voyvodes of the country. Whatever care was bestowed upon the Prince's education, he amply profited by it; he is an excellent French and Italian, as well as German and Russian scholar. He is exceptionally well informed, and on a great variety of subjects; and voracious to a degree for more information, especially concerning English laws, customs, and manners, in all of which he takes the greatest interest, and is most anxious that Englishmen should visit his country. He was good enough to have me repeatedly at his house and at his hospitable board, and he never omitted to repeat to me.

"I shall always be glad to see English gentle-men in my country; tell them, when you go back, that if they are fond of shooting, they shall have their choice of game, from an eagle to a blackbird, and from a bear to a squirrel; if they prefer fishing, I promise them trout such as they have never dreamt of,* and they shall have every assistance that I can afford them in the way of tents to camp out, and men to guide and help them."

In appearance, the Prince is tall and remarkably handsome; his hair is black, he wears both beard and moustachios, contrary to the fashion of his country, where only the latter are worn, often of immense size and length. With a commanding appearance, he still has a most benevolent expression of countenance, due to the softness of a very fine pair of eyes, and his manners are most capti-

* I was informed at Cettigne that trout were caught in the Mor-atcha of fifty or sixty pounds weight; not salmon, for the Moratcha does not go to the sea, and if it did go, there are no salmon in the Adriatic. Thinking it must be a joke, I asked several persons of standing, who all assured me that it was perfectly true. I regret that being unprovided with tackle, in addition to being short of time, I was unable to test the accuracy of these assertions, mainly in reference to my readers, because as to myself I have no reason whatever to doubt the truth, accuracy, and bona-fides of my informants; I fully accept what I heard from them, especially from my previous knowledge of the amazing number and size of the trout in the Servian rivers.

vating. He is very dignified, but at the same time most kind, without being in the least patronizing, and I was told by those who knew him best that he has a most equable temper, and that an angry word seldom was heard from him.

I had been careful before leaving the Palace to set my watch exactly to their time, so as to ensure my punctuality in the evening; and at eight p.m. to the minute, I found myself in the saloon of the Palace. The Russian Consul was there already; he was showing me the different portraits which hung round it, when the Prince walked in, in full Montenegrin costume, but without any ceremony; and a few minutes after a door was thrown open from the opposite side, when in walked the Princess, accompanied by the widow of Prince Mirko and attended by her lady-in-waiting, Mademoiselle Neukomm, all in full native costume.

Pero Pejovich had so often extolled the beauty of the Princess, that I was quite prepared to be disappointed, as is almost always the case, for anticipation seems invariably to exaggerate the reality; but on this occasion it was just the reverse. I don't think I ever saw a more beautiful creature than the lady to whom I was then introduced; tall, pale, neither thin nor stout, but beautifully formed, and with exquisite hands and arms. She wore a diamond ornament on her head, half hidden by the masses of black hair among which it was nestled, and though it shone at times like a star from among a mass of stormy clouds, it could not subdue the light which shone from her glorious dark eyes.

Dinner was instantly announced, and we proceeded to the dining-hall, a room of good size and well-furnished. The dinner, a German one, was good, the wines better. The attendance consisted of two men in black and four in native costume. The Princess, who speaks French fluently, did the honours with most winning grace; and the Prince, by his affability, at once put every one at his ease. At dinner I sat on his left, his mother being on his right, with the Russian Consul *vis-à-vis*, principally, I suppose, to facilitate her enjoyment of the conversation, as she speaks only Slave.

During the repast His Highness constantly asked me questions, sometimes about my impressions of Montenegro, which were easily enough answered, as I had nothing to recount of myself but enjoyment since I had entered his territory, having met with nothing but the most unbounded kindness and hospitality. But in his anxiety for knowledge, he often put questions which I found it difficult enough to reply to, and sometimes questions which I could not answer at all. Having spoken with admiration of the gorgeous costume of the Montenegrins, and how it set off their fine figures, he replied:

" Yes, it is very fine ; but I should be delighted to abolish it, if it were possible; they spend a great deal too much money on it."

Being simply horrified at the idea of doing away with national dress, I could not avoid expressing myself unreservedly, and I said at once that depriving a country of its costume would be simply to destroy it.

"Ah !" replied the Prince sharply, " you look upon us only from a picturesque point of view ; in fact, you would like to keep us here like a sort of menagerie of wild beasts, to come and look at us occasionally for your amusement."

The Prince was almost angry; but fortunately I had an analogous example to place before him, in our own Scottish Highlanders, who cling to their costume with such tenacity. I told him of our Highlanders, of our splendid Highland regiments, of how our Scottish nobility held by the national dress, and of how our precious Queen dressed all her boys in Highland costume; and yet we did not go to look at them as we would go to look at wild beasts in a zoological garden, but we regarded it with admiration, as an ancient national costume, associated in our minds with devoted loyalty, stirring times, and valiant deeds; as their own costume was also, which, I trusted, I should never live to see exchanged for a bad imitation of the present universally adopted French fashion, ending by saying that I was convinced that the supplanting of national costumes with imitations taken from our neighbours, was decidedly a backward step in civilization.

He questioned me very closely upon the law of

primogeniture and entail in our country, and could not understand how such a law did not produce *des jalousies terribles, et d'autres inconvenances.* I endeavoured to explain to him the present law of English entail, and how it differed from the ancient Roman law of *fidéi-commis,* which still obtains in Scotland, where entails are for ever. Still he did not like our system of primogeniture, where the eldest son, in many instances, has £100,000 per annum, and all the other children £10,000 each, representing about £400 a year. He thought it terribly unfair; indeed he could not understand how they quietly submitted to it at all; and so we got through our dinner most agreeably without the least *gêne,* while the Prince's band played some excellent music outside, under the window. This band consisted entirely of Montenegrin lads, some quite young, and considering the short time they had been learning their new profession, was wonderfully good. The bandmaster was from Prague, an excellent musician, and as he was a Czchech, he spoke a language very similar to Montenegrin, which contributed not a little to his success.

Having left the dining-room in company with the ladies, we all adjourned to the saloon, and from it to the terrace in front of the Palace, where the Prince having lit a cigarette, offered some to me and Mr. Yonin. As I hesitated to light mine, after having taken one, the Princess, who immediately guessed that my hesitation was owing to her being present, at once most kindly came forward and requested me to smoke "*de suite*," &c. I therefore lit my cigarette at once, saying with a deep bow that I dared not disobey her commands. She then bid me watch, as presently a change would suddenly take place in the aspect of the scene.

It was now quite dark, when suddenly a cannon was fired, and simultaneously, as if by magic, every window in the town, in the Palace opposite, in the monastery, in the terrace, and at every point where a candle could be stuck, was filled with lights, while the band played the grand Russian National Hymn, and the people shouted with all the power of their lungs, firing off their pistols in the air in every direction.

The illumination was so instantaneous that

the effect was charming, and coupled with the music, the enthusiastic cheering, and the booming of the cannon, which kept up a sort of "contrabasso" accompaniment to the whole, all contributed to produce a *coup de scène* never to be forgotten.

We now all withdrew to the drawing-room for coffee and tea, *à la Russe*, without cream and with a slice of lemon. I was not sorry to leave the balcony, for that firing of pistols in the air is not so innocent a pastime as might be imagined, as no Montenegrin ever dreams of loading his weapons with anything else than ball-cartridge.

The Prince again resumed his conversation with me about English customs and manners. He said, "I am told that in London one policeman, unarmed, can control a mob, while in Paris it is very different, as nothing short of loaded muskets and bayonets will do for the French."

I answered him that English mobs could be troublesome too, but that, generally speaking, owing to our constitutional respect for the majesty of the law, we came to look upon that solitary unarmed policeman as an impersonation of it, and as such he was always sure of the active assistance of all respectable citizens in the execution of his duty.

He then began to question me about the British constitution, and I never felt more posed. Irish mother-wit, however, came to the rescue, and I said, " To explain the British Constitution I should have to be a lawyer, but one of the great characteristics of it, so far as a layman like me can explain it, consists in what is called the Law of Habeas Corpus, by which no man can be imprisoned by any authority whatever without being immediately informed of the accusation against him, and brought up before the constituted authorities within twenty-four hours."

He said he had heard of that before, and thought it a grand law, but under certain circumstances he considered it might be advantageous for the king to have the power of arresting dangerous characters, upon which I told him that in certain emergencies the law of Habeas Corpus had been suspended, but that could only be done by Act of Parliament, and not by the sovereign's authority.

" In short," said he, " your Chambers are the real sovereign, the King being only the outward and visible sign of regal authority."

CHAPTER XVII.

THE firing had now ceased, and the
illumination was fading out by degrees, the band was still playing in
front of the Palace, and the full
moon was rising well up in the sky. The crowd
had increased, as we could see from the window of
the saloon, and the broad space in front of the
Palace was literally paved with heads and up-turned
faces. After looking a few minutes at that dense
mass which was swaying to and fro and gradually

getting closer and closer, the Prince asked me what I thought of their behaviour. "Most wonderfully quiet, orderly, and well behaved; but I can't help looking upon them all as so many powder kegs. One cross word, an imaginary insult, a little too much drink, one of a thousand trifling incidents, might set a spark going, and it will be wonderful indeed if among these thousands of wild and lawless men some turmoil does not arise, and when their Oriental blood is once up, and arms are at hand and ready, blood will scarcely fail to flow."

"Well," said the Prince, "I venture to say there won't be the smallest misadventure to-night, though I haven't a policeman near here, and there are probably twenty thousand armed men in and about Cettigne at this moment. Do you think there are many Sovereigns in Europe who could with safety walk about in such a crowd in one of their own capitals during a time of excitement such as this?"

"Not one, I should think," I replied.

"Then," said he, "put on your hat and come along with me."

I followed him into the lobby, where throwing a scarf about his shoulders he bid me follow him, first having told his henchman that he would go out alone.

It was now about eleven P.M., and in a few minutes we were out shouldering our way in the thickest of the crowd, making for the spot where the band was playing. It was not long before he was recognised, right and left, and now began one of the most interesting scenes I ever witnessed. Where there had been a crowd so dense that progression seemed almost an impossibility, an ample space was formed, and then one by one men of all grades approached the Prince, and, according to their rank and station, one and all saluted him in the following way—they took off their caps, and those of the lowest grades took up the edge of his coat and " literally kissed the hem of his garment ;" then those of somewhat better position kissed the same garment higher up; to others of higher rank still, the Prince extended his hand, which they kissed most reverently, and pressed to their foreheads three times ; and lastly the Chiefs and Voyvodes, almost on an equality with him, doffed their caps, while His Highness did the same, and both holding each other's right hand pressed the side of their cheek against each other. And so I accompanied him, walking through that living mass, stopping every moment either to receive some act of homage, or to caress some bold little curly-headed fellow who had squeezed and wriggled himself in to get near to his Prince, and to whom His Highness would speak a few words, asking his name and age, and where he went to school, and what he could do, to the untold pride and joy of the parents who were watching. And so we shortly made the tour of the town, coming out on the plain right in front of the monastery where many groups were busily engaged in the performance of the national dance.

The lights had now gone out, and the illumination had faded away, but the moon nearly at the full was high up in the heavens, and shining as it does not, alas! shine in these islands. The band was gone, and the only music to be heard was the native *guzla*, accompanied by the monotonous chaunt of the vocalists, interrupted occasionally by the wild piercing shriek of some dancer. The Prince made for one of the groups where apparently the dancing was most energetic, whilst I followed close on his heels. Being at once recognised, ample way was made for him, and I soon found myself alongside of him in the innermost circle of the ring.

Here I had full opportunity of observing the native Montenegrin dance, which, if not elegant, has certainly the merit of originality. How shall I describe it? In the area of that ring in which we found ourselves were five couple of dancers, who were being constantly renewed, men and women, as either became exhausted by their exertions. The dance itself did not seem to consist of any peculiar steps, but mainly in jumping with the arms extended horizontally, leaping as high as each one could opposite the other, and twirling round at the same time like dancing dervishes, whilst occasionally, as either man or woman had to give in from sheer exhaustion, they uttered a piercing shriek. Though somewhat savage and uncouth to behold, there still was a weird charm about that dance. The tall mountaineers looked taller still from their long white surtouts in the bright moonlight, and as they sprang high into the air they appeared absolutely gigantic, while the glitter of the moon's rays on the metallic ornaments of their dress and their jewelled arms produced a strange and pleasing effect. From one group the Prince passed on to another, and so through all till about one in the morning, when he turned his steps towards the Palace,

"Our dance is not an elegant one," said the Prince, "but it is characteristic; it is called the Dance of the Eagles, and its origin is thus accounted for. Many years ago the Montenegrins had no national dance, when some of the young men said, 'How is it all our neighbours have national dances of their own and we have none? Let us imagine and invent a dance; and, as our mountains are the country of the eagles, let us make it like eagles rising from the rocks, and let us scream like the young eagles.' And so they stretched out their arms and sprang into the air as high as they could, dancing their Eagle Dance, which from thenceforth became the national dance of the country."

At the gates of the Palace I made my bow, and

the Prince, putting out his hand, wished me good night, saying, "I must see you again before you leave."

In a few minutes I was in my room. I required no light, the moon was so brilliant. The night being warm, and not feeling at all sleepy from the excitement I had gone through, I lit a cigar, and leaning with my elbows on the window-sill, I looked out into the little plain where so shortly before I had been walking about. The turmoil had now greatly diminished, and in every direction I could see that preparations were being made to bivouac *à la belle étoile.* The horses that up to this time had been allowed to roam about here and there, cropping the scanty herbage, were now being collected and picketed one by one near the spot which had been selected by the owner for his own peculiar sleeping place; while the court-yard of the old Palace was also fully tenanted, and apparently by the same party I had watched in the early morning, and which, from the better style of their horses, the glitter of their equipments, and the appearance of their attendants, seemed to belong to some of the native chiefs.

By degrees the different noises ceased, and in less than an hour the whole camp was steeped in silence. Such a contrast to the noise and turmoil of an hour before, when twenty thousand people, men, women and children, were shouting, dancing, and yelling at the top of their voices!

I put on my helmet, and with a short stick in my hand, simply to keep away any snarling dog that might be inclined to give trouble, I quickly crossed the court-yard and let myself out by the gate into the plain. The moon had barely passed the zenith, and shone almost perpendicularly on the prostrate groups, who, in different attitudes of sleep, were dotted all about; some wrapped up in their strookas, more from habit than necessity, as the air was warm; some turned on their faces, some on their back with their arms outstretched; but all profoundly asleep; and such was the silence that, but for the absence of blood and mutilated limbs and broken weapons, one could easily have imagined it the field of some hard-fought fight.

I was surveying the placid scene and standing close to a magnificent mountaineer who was sleeping on his back, with his face fully upturned to the moon and his arms extended, when suddenly he awoke. In the twinkling of an eye he was on his feet and his hand on his yataghan. I don't imagine my life was the least in danger, even for a moment—but if it was, my helmet and my cigar saved me.' However, I instantly saluted him in Slave, and with a *" Sbogo Gospodin"* he returned the compliment, at the same time putting out his hand he shook mine warmly, and pointing with the other to the ancient Palace, led me away towards it, talking softly the while and smiling; but unfortunately I could not understand, and the only response I could make was by offering him a cigar, which he at once lit at mine and pro-nouncing it *" dobre,"* (good) puffed away at it with a will. At the great gate of the Palace he wished me good-night, when I begged of him by signs to take another weed, and so we parted.

The next morning being the day of the feast, I was awoke pretty early by the repeated firing of cannon just outside the gate of the Palace and in front of my window. I should have been glad to have slept a few hours longer, but the noise was too great, and my so-called Italian-speaking servant coming in at the same moment, I jumped out of bed and called out, " *Colazione !*"

I had not more than half finished, and was in the act of peeling some grand specimens of Albanian figs, when in walked Pero Pejovich, who came to tell me that the Prince and Princess, with all the notables and Voyvodes of Montenegro, would attend High Mass at ten, and that the *cortége* would pass under my windows and would be worth seeing. He added that if I liked he would take me into church and get me standing-room inside before they arrived; but he feared the crowd and the heat would be something fearful. Consequently, finding it quite hot enough already, I determined to remain where I was and enjoy the procession from my window.

I then told the Commandant of my adventure the night before. He scolded me awfully, but patted me on the back, as one would a child, and said I might have run some risk had I not been fortunately recognised as a guest of the Prince.

"Only imagine," said he, "if anything had gone wrong, the honour of Montenegro might have been compromised."

We then lit our cigars, and while waiting for mass-time, fell, as usual, into conversation about his country and its usages.

"What do you think of our Prince, and the way he goes among the people? I saw you last night with him. Did you ever see such love, such devotion, as we all have for him? But he deserves it fully. There never was such a ruler as our Prince; we would all lay down our lives for him, and be proud of the honour. If he were to call us to arms, we could muster in twelve hours, here in this plain of Cettigne, twenty thousand able men, fully armed and equipped, ready to march on any point, and that without endangering Montenegro; for we should leave twenty thousand more behind us, not so well adapted for advancing in an enemy's country, but fully competent to guard our mountain passes and protect our strongholds."

I said I hoped such a contingency might never arise; but he shook his head. The Turks, he said, hated them too much not to seek, sooner or later, for a pretext to attack them, and then he added,

"But the sooner the better; we never were so well prepared to meet them. The Turks pretend that Montenegro is an integral portion of the Ottoman Empire; we insist that we have always been free, and though often hard pressed by Ottoman forces, have never yet been conquered. What chance then is there of our coming to an understanding? My great grief, however, is to hear that England is against us and in favour of our enemies, and if it were not for the friendship which Russia has ever shown us, we might be exterminated by the infidels before you would lift a finger to prevent our utter annihilation. We cannot understand it, for we read of how England exerts herself always in favour of oppressed nationalities, and how she has even spent hundreds of millions of piastres to put down the slave trade; and yet she favours the Turks, who are the greatest supporters of slavery, against us, though our religions are almost identical, I am told. I wish more English would come to Montenegro. I think they would end by appreciating us."

These words of the Commandant made a deep impression on me.

CHAPTER XVIII.

TRULY very little is known about Montenegro and its mountaineers, and that little is very incorrect. They have been generally represented as wild, savage, bloodthirsty, thieving scoundrels, closely allied to Italian brigands and Greek palikari—if anything, worse than either. Fond of fighting for fighting's sake, and when not engaged in that amiable recreation, spending their time in strutting about in their fine clothes, peacocking in the sunshine, while those too poor to have fine trappings whiled away the weary hours and forgot their fleas and their sorrows in the tones of their national *guzla*, while the women were left to do all the labour in the fields.

Such was certainly not my impression. The part of Montenegro through which I travelled, though sterile and barren to a degree, was a wonderful specimen of what man could do when driven to it. Every little nook, where the least bit of soil could be found, among that wilderness of rocks where stones had rained from Heaven, was carefully taken advantage of; the rocks adjoining these little nooks were often removed by the most laborious exertions, and in some instances earth was scraped up here and there, and carried in small baskets to these spots, in order to increase their depth of soil. I saw clearings of so small a size as barely to admit of *one potatoe plant* or three of maize, and little fields not *one yard* in diameter!

Hard at work, cultivating the soil, I saw not only women but plenty of sturdy mountaineers.

At Niegosh I observed one of the Petrovichs, the handsome young fellow who entertained me on my way to Cettigne, superintending himself a number of men who were working in a field near his house; and the only difference I could observe between them and our own labourers was that they were all fully armed, although employed at the peaceful occupation of agriculture. They have not yet turned their yataghans into spades and reaping hooks, but they have done the next best thing by keeping the first at ease while energetically plying the others.

I have seen the Montenegrins in their own valleys and mountain fastnesses, and I utterly deny the charges brought against them. They are not lazy—leaving all the hard work to their women—that is utterly false, and the best proof I perhaps can give, lies in the self-asserting fact of the toiling colony of three thousand Montenegrin Facchini at Constantinople, well known as about the most hard-working and honest labouring men in that capital. It is true that they allow the women to do much of the heavy agricultural work, and carry heavy loads up and down the mountains;

but it must be remembered that for years past the Montenegrins, like the proscribed clans of Scotland in the last century, have been treated by their neighbours, the Turks, very little better than wild beasts. They would long ago have been exterminated, but for their indomitable courage and constant fighting, during which period, of necessity, the agricultural duties fell entirely on the decrepit old men and the women, as all men who were at all able to carry arms were engaged in fighting— and many of the women too! It must also be remembered that in all mountainous countries the women toil more heavily than in the plains, and even in civilized Italy hear what a distingnished Italian, Massimo d'Azeglio, writes:

" For example, if a faggot of wood and a bunch of chickens have to be carried down to the shore from one of the villages half way up the mountain, the labour is thus distributed in the family. The wife loads herself with the faggot of wood which weighs half a hundredweight, and the husband will take the chickens which weigh a mere nothing." The Montenegrins are not, therefore, singularly and atrociously barbarous in this respect.

Considering the small extent of the Principality and its great sterility, it is wonderful the amount of produce they are able to export, even with the disabilities under which they labour, being entirely deprived of any seaboard, though clearly entitled to one. One of the most important of their natural products, one which under favourable circumstances might be increased a thousandfold is "sumach," a substance largely used in tanning the more expensive kinds of leather. A small amount is exported to Holland, none comes to England, but a small parcel I brought over with me was declared by competent judges to be equal to the best Sicilian, which is considered the best of all sumachs.

They have vast forests of walnut trees which, under proper management and due facilities of exportation, might be rendered most productive, both as to walnut oil and timber for cabinet work. They export immense quantities of a small dried fish "*scoranza*," much used in the neighbouring Catholic and Greek countries during their religious feasts; and without further wearying my readers, I will simply add that but for the difficulties they labour under, they could export everyone of the following articles in very considerable quantities :—

Castradina (dried mutton and goat hams), honey, wax, goat and kid skins to any amount, as also martin, fox, and hare skins, together with many other substances I have forgotten.

The Prince is doing all he can to spread instruction among his people. He has established numberless schools, and as all over the Principality education is compulsory, in another generation the man or woman unable to read and write will be a phenomenon indeed in Montenegro.

The renewed booming of the cannon and the ringing of the convent bells now gave us warning that the Prince was going to hear Mass, and in a few seconds I saw the whole *cortége* pass on foot under my window. First a squad of guards, then His Highness the Prince leading the beautiful Princess, immediately accompanied by the Russian Consul in full uniform, and then a number of

Voyvodes in gorgeous costumes, while another squad of body-guards brought up the rear. They walked quickly past, and in a few minutes were lost completely to sight under the buttresses of the old Palace. The pageant was of short duration, but it was well worth seeing, even in that land of sunshine and gorgeous costumes.

Mass over, everyone turned in for his dinner and siesta. The Commandant of the Grahovo went to his own abode, and I followed the general example.

In the afternoon some wonderful foot races were to be held, but not till near sunset, when the great heat of the day would be somewhat abated. I determined therefore to fill up the space between the end of my siesta and the visit to the races, with a call on Monsignor Roganovich, the Metropolitan of Montenegro. I had brought letters of recommendation to the Archimandrite of Cettigne, and in his company I went to the monastery to pay my respects. We entered by the great gate, after crossing the threshing floor, and having crossed the court we ascended by a very rough stone staircase, which landed us in a sort of primitive cloister looking on a garden, on which opened the suite of rooms occupied by the Metropolitan.

We were at once shown in, and had not to wait many seconds before Monsignor Roganovich made his appearance. His reception was most cordial. He took me by the hand and made me sit on the divan by his side, expressing his regret that he could not converse with me except through an interpreter, owing to his not speaking any other language than Illyrian and Russian. We got on, however, remarkably well, thanks to the rapidity with which the Archimandrite almost guessed what I was going to say in Italian, translating it into Illyrian with equal rapidity. Coffee, as usual, was served up, unaccompanied however by the customary pipes, as the orthodox clergy are forbidden to smoke.

And now as I am sipping my coffee, let me endeavour to describe what I saw as my eyes wandered about. The room itself was small and low, simply white-washed, with no other furniture than one small table in front of the divan, and four rush chairs of the homeliest description.

Around the walls were a few coloured prints of saints, and the floor was utterly uncarpeted. All this simplicity, however, served to bring out in greater contrast and relief the portly figure of Monsignor Roganovich, as he sat on the divan in his ample cassock and gown of violet-purple silk. He was not a handsome man, strictly speaking, his was more a jolly countenance than a handsome one, still it was a face one liked to look at, with his grand black beard flowing down to his waist. He wore his hair in ample curls down his back as if it had never known the shears, and on his head the little Montenegrin cap of black silk. On his breast glittered the star of the Montenegrin order, and round his neck a massive gold chain, from which depended a Panagia or image of the Virgin and Child, nearly as large as a saucer, surrounded with large diamonds.

His manners were courtly and his smile most pleasing, and he gave me the idea of one who would make an excellent companion for a little dinner party of four, and who would be more in his element on the Boulevard des Italiens at Paris, than in his monastic seclusion at Cettigne. We conversed for half an hour or so when I rose to take my leave, and he gave me the Apostolic Benediction, and embraced me on both cheeks. As we walked back to the Palace, the Archimandrite told me he took great interest in the schools, which he visited daily, examining and cross-examining the students, to see that they made good use of their time.

CHAPTER XIX.

IN the afternoon I went out into the plain to see the foot races, which the Prince had told me would be very amusing.

On my way to the plain, where the races were to take place, I rambled again through the fair, and a second time got into conversation with the fellow that spoke English so well. We chatted together on many subjects, all more or less connected with the country; he praised the Montenegrins to no end, and told me he would trust them to any amount, they were so thoroughly honest and scrupulous in their dealings. He wanted me to go with him, in a couple of days after the fair was over, to the monastery of Ostrog, but my time was not my own, and I could not give myself that additional plea-sure.

It was a great disappointment, however, as Ostrog is a wonderful place, cut out of the rock, not perched on one as some of the monasteries of Mount Athos are, but partly excavated at a great height out of the face of the rock, and partly built on a ledge which the upper part of the rock overhangs. It is approached by a narrow path cut into steps, where no more than two could walk abreast, and therefore easily defended by a handful of men against any number of assailants. There is an ample supply of water in it at all times, and it is always stored with a good supply of rations, and an immense quantity of ammunition. Except by starving out the garrison, it never could be taken.

My companion wanted me then to go with him

into the interior of Northern Albania, where he was well known, and where under his protection and guidance I should have been perfectly safe ; while his knowledge of the languages, both Oriental and English, would have enabled me to make many interesting inquiries.　When I asked him about the administration of those countries by the Ottoman Government, and the opening up of the country by the projected railway from Adrianople to Novi-Bazar which has already been surveyed, he shrugged his shoulders, and then, with a toss of his head, said :—

"Railways are all very good, but they are almost useless here.　What we want is a good Government, and that we never shall have as long as this Christian country is ruled by the Turks. You talk of the progress of civilization among them ; but you simply know nothing about them. I can speak, for I have lived with them and among them from childhood ; and as to their civilization, it is simply a farce.　Even at Stamboul, among the better educated, among those who have been to Paris and London, their civilization is nothing more than the gilding of Brummagem jewelry—

the slightest rubbing will cause the copper to blush out from beneath. Civilization indeed! See what a powerful navy they possess; but let Hobart Pasha go home and take with him all his European officers, men and engineers, leaving nothing behind but pure full-blooded Turks to man it, and the entire Ottoman navy would not be a match for the smallest British ironclad. In making this disparaging statement as to the so-called civilization of Turkey, I have selected the navy as an example because in old times the Turks were able to hold their own at sea, and showed a great aptitude in naval matters; but naval science has progressed and they have remained stationary. But so it is—their civilization is a dream; their finances a colossal sham; and their final exodus from Europe, I trust, is in the very nearest distance. In fact, if all the Christians in Ottoman employ—English, French, Armenian or Greek—were to abandon their several posts, Turkey would simply collapse in six months."

I don't say that these are my opinions, but simply the clearly expressed convictions of a sharp trader who had long been intimate with European Turkey.

It wanted not much more than an hour of sunset; the western crags threw long purple shadows along the plain of Cettigne, while the rocks which bound it on the east were steeped in the richest tints of gold, and russet, and purple. Up, near to the old Palace of the Vladikas, was a splendid group of native magnates with the Prince in the midst, while ranged in a row before them were about a hundred and fifty of the most athletic men in Montenegro—competitors all in a coming foot race for a splendid pair of silver-mounted pistols, offered by His Highness to him who should first lay his hands on them. The pistols were placed on a conspicuous rock a considerable way up the cliffs on the south-west side of the plain.

The competitors may have been placed at a distance of three hundred yards from the base of those cliffs; it was, therefore, partly a flat race and partly a *"course à la montagne :"* as the Prince said, *"En Angleterre vous avez les courses au clocher,* (steeple-chases) *ici nous avons les courses*

à la montagne." The men had divested themselves of their white coats, and their belts and
armour. For an instant there was profound silence,
and then, at a given signal, off they went at a
good pace, keeping wonderfully together for the
first two hundred yards or so; then the line began
to get wavy, and with every stride more and
more fell behind, till, when they arrived at the
foot of the crags, there were not, perhaps, more
than fifty that sprang up simultaneously to the
cliffs. Then, indeed, began the real race, and
the mountaineers took to it in right earnest,
scaling the precipice like leopards. It was quite
exciting to watch the rapidity with which they
swung themselves from point to point, taking
advantage of every cleft, every rootlet, that
offered the least hold to either hand or foot.
At last, three arrived almost simultaneously at
the goal; but one, slightly in advance, made a
vigorous spring—touched the pistols first—barely
winning by a hand !

It was, without exception, the prettiest thing
by way of a race I ever saw. The whole scene
was before you like a panorama; the costumes

of the runners and the spectators; the gorgeous
tints of the setting sun; the enthusiasm of all,
together with the shouts of the multitude, rendered
it a scene never to be forgotten; and as I watched
them clambering up the cliffs in front of me,
guessing at the chances of the race, and mentally
gambling with myself on who would be the winner,
I could not help feeling a certain degree of surprise
that no betting was going on in any part of that
vast assemblage. The chances were so many, the
combinations so varied, and the probabilities so
constantly changing, that a fairer game to try the
luck of Dame Fortune could not have been
devised, and all the more, too, as all were honestly
in earnest in striving for the prize. There were
no dark horses, no sickened favourites, no hard-
pulling jockeys to bewilder the backers; all was
before you, fair and serene, and the excitement
was tremendous when some one fine mountaineer,
well in advance of the rest, maybe by five or
six yards, would suddenly lose his foothold through
the giving way of some small projection of rock
to which he was clinging, and after remaining
suspended a short time by his hands above his

head, he would eventually have to let go his hold
and drop down some few feet, losing all chance
in the race; while those who had been nearest to
him would redouble their efforts, and thus at
times the one who at first starting had seemed
the least likely to win would actually come to
be in the first flight of the race; but he, in
his turn, by some unlucky chance would slip,
and another would as instantly get on before
him.   These constant changes of chances made
the race a most exciting one; still not a bet among
the multitude of lookers-on!

One of the Prince's aide-de-camps having heard
me express surprise at the absence of all betting,
said, "Betting is quite a characteristic of you others
(*vous autres*) in England. I am told you would
bet on anything. I have heard a story of a poor
girl who once threw herself off a bridge in
London. The police-boat, fortunately, was near,
and pulled away to her rescue, when two lords
happening to pass by, stopped on the bridge for a
bet as to whether the girl would be saved or
not, and lost and won an immense sum on the
event."

I laughed, and replied,

" *Se non è vero è ben trovato.* "

After this we had a flat race for about a mile across the plains. So far as running went, it was a *flat* race indeed, and I have often seen better at an Irish country fair; but it was well worth seeing from the rich colouring of the costumes of those taking part in it, as they ran with their clothes on; and as every one was eligible to compete, and not Montenegrins alone, the effect was most singular and picturesque. The prize was in this case also a pair of silver-mounted Turkish pistols, given by the Prince, and I was glad to hear that the winner was a Montenegrin.

In the evening I had the honour of dining at the Palace, when the Prince again asked me many questions concerning England, its habits and customs, of which, although he had read much in French books, he knew absolutely nothing.

We again spoke about the law of primogeniture, about which he could not exactly make up his mind, and could not understand how it did not produce disastrous occurrences in families. He understood, however, quite well what I explained to him concerning the Law of Habeas Corpus, and again declared it to be a grand institution, *so far as the people were concerned.*

I left at a late hour, after spending a most delightful evening, and as I went back to my rooms to pack my small valise for my early start next morning, I felt an undefinable regret at leaving Tchernagora and its interesting moun taineers. I had enjoyed among them a courteous hospitality and a patriarchal welcome, the prominent characteristics of which will, I fear, before very long disappear under the pressure and *vis a tergo* of our so-called European civilization. I should like, above all things, to visit them again; but should it never be my lot to enjoy that pleasure, I cannot take leave of Montenegro without expressing my deep sense of the cordial reception I met with there on every side.

CHAPTER XX.

A S the clock struck three in the morning of the 15th of July, 1873, the guide walked into my room to say it was time to start; at the same moment my servant brought me in a cup of *café-au-lait* with some hot toast. My toilette was soon made, and my breakfast swallowed, and I moved away from Cettigne as the clock chimed the half-hour after three.

It was still night, but not dark, as the moon had not yet set, and a band of rose-coloured light streaked the Eastern horizon. We started at a rapid trot, startling the echoes up the solitary and deserted street of Cettigne, and we never slackened our pace till we came to the verge of the little plain in which it is situated, when the path up the ravine which led westward to the Adriatic became so rugged that we were compelled to walk our horses, and in less than half-an-hour more had to dismount and proceed on foot.

In a short time we reached the crest of the range which encircles the Plains of Cettigne, and the track becoming less precipitous, we remounted ; but before leaving the spot I turned my horse round to have a last look at that mountain capital where I had been so hospitably entertained, and where, most probably, I might never have the pleasure of being again.

I was now standing on the highest point of the pass, and I enjoyed a most delightful view. The sun was just in the act of rising. My back was to the Adriatic, while my face was turned to the East. At my feet lay the Plain of Cettigne, girt round on all sides with precipitous rocks and mountains. Beyond the plain, far in the hazy horizon—not foggy—but rendered slightly indistinct by a faint cobalt haze, I could see the Lake of Skodra glittering in the morning sun with the thin silver streak of the Zeta river losing itself in it, while in the still further distance I could perceive the faintest outline of the Albanian mountains. Right and left, as far as the eye could reach, nothing but rocky peaks and precipices met the view—nothing but rocks with here and there a few scanty bushes, on which were browsing large herds of goats tended by wild-looking men, carrying round their waist, as usual, the inevitable arsenal of weapons, and the long Albanian gun over their shoulders.

I would have lingered over this scene, and I was already thinking of getting down and sketching it, when the guide remonstrated against any such proceeding on my part. "It was very near the dog days," he said, "and to be caught by the noon-day sun on those bare rocks, was a thing to be avoided;" so I was compelled to move on, after giving another long look at the picture to which I was about to turn my back.

The guide was right; the track was abominable, and we could only proceed at a slow pace. At the same time, the sun was gaining strength with every inch it rose above the horizon, and by the time we reached the *clachan* of Niegosh, its rays come down upon us like molten lead; but my old helmet was proof against them, and an excellent protection, while the faint breeze which came up from the Adriatic prevented all feeling of oppression.

At Niegosh, where a week before I had been so kindly entertained by young Pejovich, we rested five minutes. I did not even dismount, but the guide went into the very primitive khan to light his pipe; but, by the way, he smacked his lips on coming out, I suspect a glass of wodky was not forgotten, while the fire for his pipe was being handed to him.

After a little, the path again became im-practicable for riding, so I had to dismount and walk, though the heat was something marvellous (I afterwards heard from Signor Jackschich that in Cattaro, in the shade, the thermometer stood at 33° Reaumur at four o'clock in the afternoon—about 105° Fahrenheit. After some difficult scrambling, when I sorely felt the want of the stout arm of Pero Pejovich, we reached the fountain, and here we rested ten minutes; then having remounted, we soon arrived at the top of the *scala*, with the Adriatic before us and Cattaro hundreds of feet down below.

It seemed now as if I should be at the end of my journey in a few minutes; the road was all before me, and I could count the zig-zags as they unfolded themselves on the face of the rock, still they seemed as if they would never come to an end. I counted one, two, three, twenty, thirty, fifty, up to one hundred bends, and still more appeared beneath me, so at last I gave it up through sheer exhaustion.

Everything, however, has an end eventually, and so the apparently interminable Scala di Cattaro came to an end also. How I got on during the last few turns and twists I forget— I was in a sort of doze; all I remember is finding myself suddenly among those heavenly

mulberry trees of the Esplanade, and hearing the friendly sound of Signor Jackschich's
welcome.

Cattaro is innocent of either inn, hotel,
khan, or caravansary, but good accommodation had been prepared for me inside the
town. I therefore rode on to the gate where I
had to dismount, as no horse is allowed to enter,
just as no carriage *can enter* the narrow gateway.

The Bocchesi (as the natives call themselves)
have one cause of heart-burning and envy,
less than we in our country; there are
no carriage-people in Cattaro to look down
upon *you* who have to trudge on foot,
and the nearest approach to anything of the
sort is an antique sedan-chair mounted on wheels
exactly like the celebrated old *push* at Hampton
Court, which was occasionally brought into requisition on gala days, when such happened to be
wet ones also.

Having reached my rooms I quickly made
my toilet, and then returned to the mulberries,
under whose welcome shade I made an excellent

breakfast and lunch in one, while many of the natives were taking their dinner.

My further steps became now somewhat uncertain. I thought I should have found the steamer here to take me down the Adriatic, but I had miscalculated; it was not due till the following day. So I determined on resting in Cattaro till evening, and then riding across the isthmus (about eighteen miles only) to Budua, where Baron von Heydeg was quartered, and picking up the steamer when it would call there in a couple of days. I at once telegraphed to Heydeg that I was going, in order that the officer on guard might open the gates for me on arrival, as no one is let in or out of Budua after sunset, without an order from the Commandant. Then I went to my room, and being fairly tired, I threw myself on the bed and slept.

It was about half-past three when I was awoke by some one knocking at my door, and to my surprise, in walked Mr. Yonin, the Russian Consul. I had forgotten to mention that we had agreed to travel from Cettigne together, and were to have met in the street opposite the Palace at three A.M.; but the servants had forgotten to call him, and when after waiting half an hour he did not come, and the guards on duty would not allow my guide to knock at the Palace gate, I started without him, thinking he had changed his mind. He had breakfasted late and then ridden to Cattaro in the middle of the day in order to catch the steamer for Ragusa that was to leave the same evening. I told him how long I had waited, and how I had tried in vain to get the sentinels to allow us to knock. He could only lament his misfortune, as, mopping his face, he added, "I assure you the heat on those bare rocks was something to be remembered all one's life." We then arranged to dine together at five o'clock before parting.

Punctual to the hour appointed, we met on the *marina*. The heat of the day had considerably diminished, for although the sun was still high in the horizon, it had long ago set for the good folks at Cattaro, as the city being built at the foot of the mountains looking to the West, and having a range of high cliffs in front of it, behind which the sun sinks long before it dips into the Adriatic, sunset at Cattaro occurs hours earlier than at any other place on the Adriatic. In Summer this is a great advantage, as it enables the inhabitants to walk out in the shade on the *marina* at a much earlier hour, the opposite cliffs protecting them from the hot rays of the sun, and at the same time affording them a sort of twilight, elsewhere unknown in those latitudes; but in Winter it must be very gloomy, as the rising sun being shut out by the rocks and mountains of Montenegro till near eleven o'clock in the morning, and again disappearing so early in the afternoon, reduces the actual day to as short a space as in the latitude of St. Petersburg.

Availing themselves of the comparative coolness of the hour, the *beau monde* of that primitive little place, among which the Bishop and the Commandant of the garrison were conspicuous, had turned out for their evening promenade, and the esplanade presented quite a gay appearance. I ordered the horses for seven o'clock, and then we went to look for our dinner at the café; but here something of a difficulty arose. The Bocchesi dine at twelve noon, or at one at latest, and sup at nine, no one ever thinking of a meal at five! so that nothing was ready. The cook, however, was equal to the emergency, and in fifteen minutes served us up a most excellent and varied dinner, to which we were about to sit down and do ample justice, when who should turn up but Pero Pejovich!

He was returning to his post in the Grahovo, and found it easier to get to it by coming round to Cattaro first, then going by sea to Risano and thence, as it were, coming back on his own steps, thus going a round of something like four times the direct distance. This will convey some idea of the difficulties to be encountered in endeavouring to cross some of the rocky regions of Montenegro.

I was delighted at seeing him again; we all dined together, and enjoyed ourselves immensely notwithstanding the heat. After dinner, Pero Pejovich pulled out from among the ample folds of his sash some Trebigne tobacco, which had never seen the countenance of a Custom House officer, and we set to work to make cigarettes, when we were joined by Signor Jackschich and Signor Radanovich, the Prince's Agent at Cattaro. Coffee and maraschino were brought out, fresh relays of cigarettes were manufactured, and we could have enjoyed ourselves for hours more, but the inexorable bell of the steamer rang out a summons that bade Mr. Yonin prepare for departure, while the increasing darkness served to remind myself that I had yet a journey before me ere I should be able to lie down to rest.

We stood up reluctantly, and in a body accompanied the Russian Consul to the steamer, and there bade him adieu, probably for ever; though who can tell? I have had at times the most unexpected *rencontres* in the most unlikely places. I first met him at Ragusa, where also I made my first acquaintance with Mr. Paton, now unfortunately no more; both very able and highly educated men, yet they seemed not to appreciate each other as they might have done, perhaps from the diametrical opposition of their political views.

Poor Paton is lost to us for ever, and we shall never have a better member of our Consular service; a shrewd, sagacious man, and a first-rate Oriental scholar.

As to Mr. Yonin, I trust I may yet meet him, and renew some of the pleasant hours I spent with him.

CHAPTER XXI.

THE twilight of Cattaro was fast merging into darkness when I returned with my companions to the esplanade, where my horses were ready to take me on to Budua. Our adieux were short but cordial, and in a few minutes I was cantering away in company with Signor Jackschich, who lives in a villa a couple of miles away from Cattaro.

If the tracks and paths of Montenegro are rugged and wild, the beautiful road we were now travelling on made ample amends for the discomfort I had endured in riding during the last few days. As we passed Signor Jackschich's villa, I insisted on his remaining there, or his courtesy would have induced him to keep me company ever so much further on; so wishing him adieu for the twentieth time, I lit my cigar, and sticking spurs into my pony, cantered away on my road to Budua. The ride was not interesting. I started too late; I should have remembered that in those latitudes, except at Cattaro, there is no twilight.

On leaving Cattaro the road is at first directly south, leading across the isthmus of the peninsula which forms the western shore of the gulf of that name. Having reached the sea, it continues to skirt the Adriatic, except in those places where to avoid rounding a headland it runs inland straight across the base of the promontory.

The night was fine, and we got on famously, but whether in consequence of the good dinner, or the genial sensation produced by the atmosphere, or the early hour I had risen in the morning, when it came to be about eleven o'clock an indescribable feeling of lassitude and intense sleepiness came over me. I would have given anything to lie down even for half-an-hour; but it was out of the question, as we were at that time crossing a sort of marsh, and there was not a dry spot to lie down on. So I was compelled to ride on; but I suspect I dozed, and then during those moments of extreme lassitude and prostration, when my vital powers were standing at their lowest, I fear I imbibed some of those zymotic germs, some malarious molecules, which a few days later manifested themselves by a smart attack of fever. Thanks, however, to a good constitution and a few doses of quinine, I was able to cut it short in three days, though it stuck to me for a little while longer in the shape of an indescribable sort of *malaise.*

At one o'clock a.m., we reached the gates of Budua, where I was met by Baron Heydeg and Signor Marco Medin. Heydeg was an officer quartered with his regiment at Budua, whose acquaintance I had made at Pola, and with whom

I had subsequently travelled. Medin was a native of Budua, who had left his country many years before, had made money in California, had married there a buxom Irish girl, a native of Ballinrobe, and had now returned, a rich man, to end his days among his relations in Dalmatia.

They had been waiting for me a long time, and had walked some miles on the road to Cattaro to meet me, but were beginning to think I was not going to keep my word.

We were soon seated together at a comfortable supper, and at half-past two a.m. I was finally allowed to retire to my bed, which Medin had kindly procured for me in a private house—because here, as in Cattaro, there is no hotel of any kind.

Tired and sleepy as I was, I passed but an in-different night, for, notwithstanding that my room had two large windows overlooking the sea, and that I kept them both open, the heat was perfectly stifling.

I was just thinking of going out the next morning about ten, when in walked the Baron and Signor Medin, and we at once adjourned for breakfast at the same place where we had supped the previous night; I say place, as it was neither an inn nor a *café*. How shall I describe it? The following is the way we got at it, anyhow. In the main street of Budua, near to the land gate, on the left hand as you come in, you meet with five rugged stone steps, flanked by a shaky single iron railing. These lead up to a strong wooden door, which at some period of its existence may have enjoyed the privilege of paint, but of which no trace remains at the present moment, not even enough to enable one to make a guess at the colour it once enjoyed.

Entering by this door, I found myself in a stuffy, dirty hall, "*a terreno*" pervaded by a multitude of vile smells, one more awful than the other, but all so dovetailed and commingled that it was perfectly impossible to tell what the composition was. Turning sharp to the left, we mounted a steep stone staircase, at the top of which we were greeted by the same odour that had met us on entering, in which now the smell of assafœtida and garlic clearly predominated. We found ourselves in the kitchen of the establishment, over which reigned supreme a good-humoured, fat German *Frau* of fifty or more, assisted by two bright-eyed, sharp-looking Dalmatian lads, be-grimed with dirt and shining with grease and perspiration. The *Frau* piloted us through this kitchen, where the heat must have been 110°, if not more, and brought us into the dining-room, a pretty good-sized room with windows round the three sides of it, the furniture consisting solely of one long deal table down the middle, and a score of rush-bottomed chairs around it. At this table were seated a dozen or so of German officers demolishing their "early bit."

I was here received by the *Frau's* worse half, a portly man of sixty or thereabouts. His coat was off, but he had on instead a huge pair of silver spectacles. He at once showed me to my seat at the table, when I apologised, through the Baron, to the officers for disturbing them at their break-fast.

Notwithstanding the unpromising condition of things, the breakfast was excellent; but mine host in the shirt sleeves, with whom I kept up a running conversation in Italian, was even better.

An Italian by birth and education (for he was very well educated), he had rambled all over the Austrian dominions and the Turkish provinces in Europe. He had forgotten most of his native tongue without learning any other, and the jargon he spoke was something marvellous. Still, he varied this *pot-pourri* according to the nationality of those he addressed. The foundation was always Italian, but if he spoke to an Austrian the German element would predominate, while if he spoke to a Montenegrin the Slave would be in the ascendant. He was a most amusing character, and combined in himself the functions of doctor, dentist and apothecary, as well as that of keeper of a restaurant in Budua—hence the villainous combination of the odours of a scullery, a kitchen, and a pharmacy.

In spite of his griminess and the vile odours, I had some very pleasant conversation with him. I found him very well informed, and he gave me a most interesting account of the last descent of the Montenegrins. He had a most unconquerable horror of my favourite mountaineers, and believed there could be no peace nor prosperity in that part of the world until they should be all exterminated.

Having finished our breakfast, Heydeg and I strolled outside the walls to where the market is held under some magnificent old carob trees, and there, as at Cattaro, were numbers of Montenegrins disposing of their produce. Here we had some delicious fresh figs, and then lighting our cigars we went round the old fortifications, which are now only just sufficient for protection at night against any sudden incursion of the wild tribes of the interior. Then we had a good bathe in a most delicious little cove, entirely girt round with rocks, and with a sandy bottom that felt like velvet under our feet. We then again lit another cigar, and started on a tour of exploration through this old town.

Budua, situated at the extreme end of Dalmatia, in what used to be called Northern Albania, is the last Austrian city on the coast of the Adriatic. It is built on a low rocky promontory, and possesses no interest, save in its picturesque appearance, which it derives from its mediæval walls and machicolated towers—useless, indeed, against a civilized enemy, but still offering some protection against possible irruptions from Albanian freebooters. It is especially picturesque as seen from the sea, with its rugged background of naked mountains. Immediately about it there is some cultivation on the narrow strip of land which lies between the mountains and the sea; and corn, vines, olive trees, and mulberries for the rearing of silk-worms, are diligently grown.

Inside, it is not attractive — its streets are extremely narrow, no more than six feet wide in many instances; they are, however, well paved, and would do well enough, were it not for the utter disregard to cleanliness and drainage. Still there are some wealthy people living there, and many of the houses are very good and substantial. There are several good shops, (perhaps the word stores would best describe them), where a brisk trade seemed to be carried on. The Baron and I poked our way through all the nooks and crannies of the place. We found nothing to invite attention, but a great deal to shock the sight, and even the sense of smell. So we hurried on and went to pay a visit to my buxom Ballinrobe friend, who had not only quite forgotten her ancestral brogue, but had actually exchanged it for a decided American accent, which, to my ears, was not an improvement. She offered us neither English tea nor Irish whiskey punch, but gave us some delicious lemonade and maraschino ; and showed by her manner that, if the brogue was gone, the hearty Irish welcome was there still.

From thence I went with the Baron to his own little apartment, which opened on to an enchanting little terrace, covered over with a grand "*pergola*" of vines, under whose refreshing shade we smoked away the time till we should go to dinner.

We had not been long enjoying an excellent repast at our pharmaceutical (deuced hard name to spell, by-the-by) restaurant when we were informed that the steamer for Corfu was entering the harbour, and would leave in two hours.

The time for parting had come at last, fresh bottles were tapped, and we all drank each others' health, and a happy journey to me amidst noisy demonstrations and much clinking of glasses. Dinner being at last completed, we all arose and walked in a body to the Mole, where, my luggage having preceded me, I went at once on board. There was no time for lengthy adieux, the steamer was whistling, and almost while we were shaking hands she cast off her moorings, and we were off.

# CHAPTER XXII.

AFTER leaving Budua we kept close in shore, enjoying the wild rugged scenery of the Dalmatian coast till we reached Antivari, where we first came into immediate contact with the Turks on their own Ottoman soil. The first impression, I must confess, was certainly not a favourable one.

Should any one of my readers, with a bias in

favour of Ottomans and Ottoman rule, ever determine on visiting Turkey, let him not receive his
first impression of that empire by a visit to
Antivari. A few wretched hovels, a miserable
white-washed house, with a small and dirty red
flag over it; a group of miserably-dressed, vile-
countenanced, ragamuffin - looking soldiers, in
baggy blue trousers and crimson fezzes, constituted all the features of the place. The
town of Antivari itself, I heard, was a few
miles inland, but if one may judge of the town
from its villainous port, it must be wretched in the
extreme.

The steamer remained here a couple of hours
to land goods and take in passengers, but as the
heat was excessive and the prospect of the country
most unpromising, I made no attempt to land. I
did not however lack entertainment, and while I
lounged over the bulwarks on the shady side
of the steamer, I amused myself pitching half-
francs into the water, which was of very considerable depth and of the clearest and limpidest
blue, to half a score or so of lads and small boys
who were swimming, and diving, and treading the

water in the most surprising manner; they seemed just as much at home in the sea as on the land, and fetched up the coins from the bottom as easily as I could have picked them up from the deck.

When tired of looking at the swimmers, I turned to watch the new arrivals, of which we had a considerable number, all Orientals, and almost all deck passengers. The first which caught my eye, coming up the side of the steamer, was a wretched-looking, squalid creature, dressed in rags, but most picturesque withal. He was small, slight, and extremely dark, just short of black, but with distinctly Caucasian features, not a negroid by any means. He had a small bundle over his shoulders, and in his right hand he carried a short lance, with a very bright steel head, ornamented with a few lines of Damascene work in gold. His head was covered with a somewhat conical-shaped cap, encircled with a scanty and very ragged green turban, while at his side he carried a moderate sized bottle-gourd. He was a very singular looking being, and all I could make out through

the captain was that he thought he was a
dervish returning home from visiting some
sacred shrine in Mahomedan Europe. As
to his home, he suspected from his costume
it might be in Kurdistan, but it was very
much guess work, as the Captain spoke neither
Arabic nor Turkish.

Another interesting group consisted of three
gaily dressed Orientals, in bag trousers tight at
the knees, turban, and highly embroidered jackets.
They made their way to the quarter-deck abaft
the paddle box, and were about being summarily
ejected by the steward in consequence of being
deck passengers, when I interposed, and got him
to let them stay for a while. They perfectly
well understood that it was owing to my inter-
ference they were allowed to remain, and so we
knocked up a sort of acquaintance, and carried
on a lame, very lame conversation by the help
of the youngest, who could speak a very few
words of Italian. I could not make out any
thing about them, whence they came, or whither
they were going, but from their features I
could easily see they were Asiatics, Arabs most

probably, and the youngest, who was also the lightest in colour, had three scars on each cheek, not unlike in shape to our broad arrow.

How I longed for a knowledge of Arabic, how I envied Captain Burton! If he had been there we should at once have known all about them, and the dervish and everyone else, including a tall, handsome Soudani slave, who kept grinning and showing his teeth from ear to ear, while I was carrying on my lame conversation with the Arabs.

Up to this point, Italian and German had enabled me to get on famously; but now that I was getting among Asiatics, although I was still in Europe, I felt my utter helplessness, and the absolute necessity for a knowledge of the language of the Koran, for those who wish to visit the East with pleasure and profit.

The whole deck forward was encumbered with passengers. In one corner seated on a pile of luggage, but well bolstered up by rolls of Persian carpets, was a most truculent-looking

Oriental, attended by an intelligent-looking young negro, with a most astonishing Caucasian type of countenance. He wore nothing but a white calico sort of shirt with loose sleeves, and a string of red beads round his neck. He had none of the characteristics of the negro except the colour; had I known anything of Arabic, I could most probably have learnt something about his origin.

In another corner of the deck a Mahomedan merchant (as I was informed he was) had contrived to screen off a place for himself and his family, one of whom, about three years old, was sprawling stark naked on a rug in the broiling sun, while a closely veiled female, his mother I suppose, was chasing small deer all over his person, which was closely spotted as if with measles — but they were only bites!

Quite at the prow of the vessel, somewhat apart, and separated from the rest, was a military officer, evidently of some considerable rank, if one could judge by the orders and stars fastened to his breast, his handsome hilted sabre, and his patent leather boots. He was a heavy morose-looking man of about fifty, with close cropped black beard, blue Turkish uniform, and crimson fez. I was told he was a real pasha, and had with him a suite of two officers and half a dozen soldiers. He was only a deck passenger like the others; but whether he travelled so from poverty, from motives of economy, or from scorning to associate with the hated and *envied* Nazarenes, I cannot tell, though I strongly suspect that genuine impecuniosity was the real cause of it.

The Turkish troops I saw in this part of Albania were the most wretched specimens I ever witnessed, small, mean, dirty, disreputable-looking in the extreme, and their officers matched them to perfection. Having remarked on their appearance, I was told by the captain of the steamer not to form an opinion of the Ottoman army by such samples, as they always sent their worst regiments to Albania, and that these wretched troops, both officers and men, were always months in arrears of pay.

At last every one was on board, the last package was hoisted over the side, and again we were steaming down southwards. The afternoon was very enjoyable, the heat much less, and as the number of cabin passengers was small, we were able to have our supper on deck, which we enjoyed immensely.

After the meal was concluded, I again went forward among the natives, and soon made friends with many of the dusky passengers by means of a few signs; but our conversation was not lively—signs and gesticulations and dumb show were the principal means of conversation—of language we made little or no use. Had I known ever so little of Arabic we could have got on fairly enough—the pantomime of these Orientals being so wonderfully expressive. So I returned to the quarter-deck, where I had some coffee with the captain, and then feeling tired, I went down to my *camerino*, and was soon asleep.

On awaking the next morning I found we were at anchor opposite the town and fortress of Castel Durazzo, telling of its Venetian origin by its name. Here we remained a few hours, but the place did not look attractive, and as I did not feel quite "the thing," I did not go on shore, but remained on deck looking at the motley groups as they passed up and down. Again we had the usual interchange of passengers and goods, and after a few hours' delay we were just about steaming away when the return steamer from Corfu came alongside of us.

As chance would have it, it turned out to be the very boat which had brought me down to Cattaro ; and no sooner did the captain spy me out on deck than he shouted that the quarantine had been declared at Corfu against all vessels coming from Trieste, and that if I went on I should be detained to perform fourteen days of quarantine in the Lazzaretto, instead of being allowed to continue my journey on to Constantinople. I asked him to come over, which he did at once, and having held a consultation with the other captain, who entirely agreed with him that I should most certainly be detained a fortnight at Corfu, and be compelled to perform my quarantine in the Lazzaretto, I determined on returning to Trieste. Fourteen days in a Lazzaretto anywhere would be a severe ordeal, but fourteen days of such an imprisonment during the dog-days at Corfu could not possibly have been faced ; it would not only have been a severe trial of patience in every shape and form, but might have been conducive to serious illness.

There was no time to be lost, so my luggage was at once put into the captain's boat, and in a few minutes I again found myself on board the old steamer, where Giovanni, the steward, greeted me as if I had been an old friend.

At sunset we steamed away northward from Castel Durazzo. The captain was delighted to see me again, and Giovanni was most affable, doing his utmost to promote my happiness. But like Rachel of old I would not be comforted, all my plans were thoroughly upset; I could not bring myself to make fresh arrangements. I was turning my back on my beloved South and I was retracing my steps—both things I utterly detested. But *non ci era rimedio*, the quarantine and the Lazzaretto I could not face, so there was nothing else to do but resign oneself to the fates.

The next morning we came abreast of Budua, but I did not land as I did not feel well. I screwed up my courage, however, and attempted a little sketch of its castle and harbour, with its blue sea and its background of rocky mountains. After a little, and just as we were leaving the place, I felt worse, so I took some medicine and went to lie down. In two hours more I was in high fever, with a racking pain in my head and back, and I felt my mind almost wandering. We reached the Bocche that evening, but the beauties of the Fjord were lost to me—I lay in my cabin prostrated. Giovanni came instantly to see me, trying to comfort me by telling me I had only caught "*la febbre*," and that I should send for the doctor at Cattaro to get myself bled, and take quinine, when I should be all right. I think that the idea of Giovanni's bringing a doctor and having me bled, *nolens volens*, roused me up. I made myself some tea, and just as we reached Cattaro I felt much better — the fever had abated, and now, said I, is the time to take the quinine.

I had brought lots of it with me, so I measured out as much as I could pile upon a shilling, and bolted it. It certainly cut short the disease, as the fever did not set in again; but I was not well for many days after, and even when I arrived at Trieste I felt quite weak and out of sorts.

The next morning early we left Cattaro, and in the afternoon got to Gravosa. I felt somewhat better, and hearing that Consul Paton, who was then alive, and his family were in a villa just opposite to where the steamer was moored, I took a boat and spent two delightful hours with them, till the steam-whistle told me how quickly the time had flown. I reluctantly made my adieux, and soon was steaming out of the harbour.

It wanted scarcely an hour of sunset: the sun was low in the horizon — all the lights and shades were the more intensely marked, while the constantly changing tints, from brightest rose and golden yellow to the deepest violets and blues, created such a fairy scene that I would not venture to describe it.

I was in the fullest enjoyment of that sunset, gazing on where the sun was just dipping into the sea, sending a flood of golden light along the surface from himself to us, when the captain tapped me on the shoulder, saying, "*Vada giù*, you had *la febbre* last night; don't expose yourself to the air *al tramonto*;" so I took his advice, and went down below, notwithstanding the heat, and so ended the 23rd day of July!

The following day saw us at Lesina and at Curzola, and again at Lissa. The day after brought us abreast of Spalato, where again I enjoyed a couple of hours' ramble among those glorious ruins. Then we cruised through the countless islands near the mouth of the Quarnero, and finally reached Trieste, where, after having enjoyed two pleasant days with Captain Burton and his charming and talented lady, I turned my steps towards home.

Here I take my leave of the reader. If he shall be disappointed with my style and my many short-comings I shall not be surprised; but I shall be disappointed indeed if, following a somewhat similar track to the one I have been tracing, only penetrating, if possible, more into Servia proper, and going across it from the Danube to the Adriatic, he shall not feel himself amply repaid by having taken my advice in visiting those countries which I have endeavoured to describe.

THE END.

London: Printed by A. Schulze, 13, Poland Street.

www.ingramcontent.com/pod-product-compliance
Lightning Source LLC
Chambersburg PA
CBHW031028120726
47905CB00007B/2087